PRODUCTIVE *intuition*

CONNECTING TO THE SUBTLE

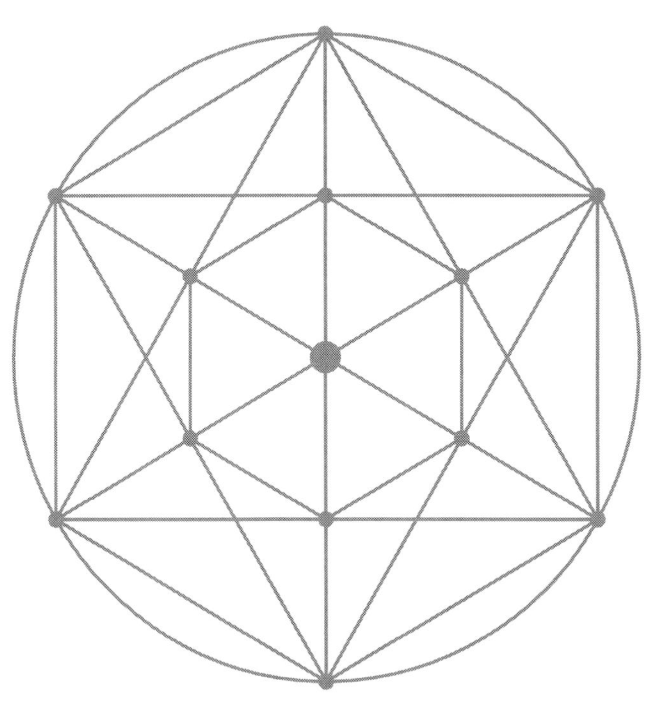

AdaPia d'Errico

Dear Lexi,

It's been a pleasure getting to know you and I am looking forward to more of that!

Adapia

To my husband, partner and soulmate, Andrew

In gratitude for his encouragement and inquisitiveness,
and for teaching me how to live with a fully open heart.

Table of Contents

Introduction:
A Portal to Your Sovereignty

Any time we open a book we unlock a doorway within ourselves. If we choose to walk through this door, we are transformed. This is the power of the wisdom this book holds: it *will* change how you experience the world.

While you are still you, by opening and reading this book you've gained access to your inner authority. You're expanded, centered, and more embodied. You're present with the challenges and conflicts in your life and you trust your ability to carve a path forward. You feel confident in your ability to execute on the opportunities that life presents you. If this sounds like the right place to start the next phase of your journey, then know that I am here to support you in unlocking your deepest power: the productive intuition that potentiates your highest self.

Intuition is both immanent and transcendent. Inner authority emerges when we trust our embodied wisdom and act with intention. The way I wrote this book is similar to how I run my Circles and live my life: I have invited you in fully to witness my journey and benefit from the tools and wisdom I've gathered along the way. No matter where this finds you in space and time, trust that we are on this journey together. For this is my story, too. This book is an honest examination of what it took to live my life with conviction and courage, to stand tall and share my truth with the world. It is an exploration of the subtle through science, story, and the senses.

It's common for us all to see our situations in a different light from others. It is one of the reasons we seek advice in the first place, to gain a different perspective. This book is meant to be a conversation with you. It is my truth in action. It is also an invitation for you to step in and interact with the content here; to make the most of the practices I share. I'm not holding back and neither should you. This space is designed to facilitate collective healing, unlock your total sovereignty, and empower you to stand tall as your divine self. It is the same way I facilitate transformation with individuals, communities, and companies: by inviting inquiry and exchange; by promoting active engagement and practice with the methods and techniques.

As you move through this book, reflect on your own life and what these insights and experiences trigger for you. You might find that you agree with me, and you might find that you dislike my way of doing things. I'm not concerned about how you feel but rather what you *do* with the emotional data points. Do you listen more deeply to yourself? Do you get curious about what my reflection brings up in you? Are you willing to ask yourself where you have given away your power?

If my story is a mirror for you, then I have succeeded in my service to the world. The process of awakening is painful, confusing, and challenging – I know this firsthand. It has never been easy, and anyone who has been through the portal knows this. Yet we live in a world where self-help and self-care are promoted like spiritual pills that can be bought on social media and used to escape the actual work ahead. The online tide of new age gurus, business goddesses, and the "high vibe tribes" has diluted a critical conversation that needs to be had. Our world is going through a massive restructuring, and if you are alive then you are being called into devoted attention and dedicated action.

Branded wokeness is working against itself. We are mistaking performance for practice. What is intended to heal is instead confusing the truth at the heart of the matter: that we are here to heal ourselves. There are many pathways and methodologies being promoted and the challenge people are faced with is to critically discern what's real and what's spiritual snake oil – and it's not always easy to know until you test it for yourself. And believe me – I have.

The new world is calling us forward into our highest alignment and it's not as cute as social media makes it out to be. Sometimes it's excruciating. But within the crucible of our awakening, we rise to meet ourselves, and this is where your true power lives: in accepting and owning all of you.

Ready or not, you are awakening. This is why you picked up this book and why it caught your attention. You are awakening because you are alive. We are designed to evolve into what we already are; to remember what exists at the center of ourselves. Thankfully, the path to actualization is lined with tests: challenges that are opportunities in disguise. Because it is when we face these challenges head-on that we witness ourselves rise.

This has been my path as a conscious business leader. When we begin to reclaim power and take up more space, we are tested. Life wants to know whether we are ready to choose differently. Having been through my share of massive tests and painful challenges, I am here to guide those who are also on the warrior path of awakened leadership. As a successful professional, I have over-exerted myself to get to the pinnacle of my career, then leave it all to pursue my passion and "fail." I've had very personal truths go viral and had to navigate online trolling and the impact of millions of eyes on my life choices. The best news? The blows have only served to strengthen me. These tests ultimately served the highest good by inviting me to step into my most sovereign self. It was here that I learned how to flow into conscious action from my heart.

The heart–not your mind–is the essence of inner authority, for the heart is the throne of pure power and potential. It is the most valuable ally you have in the process of actualizing your true self. When we are not connected to this divine intelligence center it is easy to get blown around by our addictive whims and untethered emotions; by the projected expectations or loud opinions of other things in our orbit.

We live in a world of noise and this makes it harder to hear the subtle teachings of our inspired center. We live in an era of increasing fragmentation, where discerning "truth" becomes even more challenging. We are all burned out on too much social media and the unconscious consumption of mindless content. Besides–something is missing from that conversation: the heart.

Creating sacred space in our life to honor what is true for us is a ritual that spans centuries. This is why humans have gathered in circles for millennia: to foster spaces where we can unplug from the chaos and come together. To elevate our spirits when we feel overextended in every corner of our lives. The teachings you'll find in this book began to cohere in my Circles of Sovereignty as I integrated the lessons and learnings of my awakening. It was also here that I was held through my dark night of the soul by my sisters, friends, and sometimes total strangers, for that is the nature of the circle: it invites us into the center of ourselves to be real and heal. One of the most important teachings that my circle has taught me is about wholeness. I have experienced firsthand how the empowered response is to meet life's challenges and uncertainty with all of me.

I don't presume to heal anyone. I offer my insights as an invitation to enter your own sacred space and reflect on what life is offering you. If my lessons can shed light on an area of your life that's keeping you stuck, then the magic of the circle is working in your life. We all have answers for one another.

Sovereignty—or as I like to think of it, our inner authority—gives us a center no matter what is happening around us. It is the most powerful tool you can carry on the path. If you are reading this book, then personal authority is what you seek. You haven't found what you were looking for outside yourself and are about to find where it's always been - within. This is what my journey has taught me: the art of holding my sovereign space. It is here that I have learned how to be whole and walk with life from that place of trust.

I have developed an alliance with my heart and now I walk in honor. That's all a warrior is, in the end. Warriors lead with love and wisdom and only battle as a last resort. This path has shown me that it's not actually about fighting your way forward—and believe me, I learned this the hard way. There's no magic wand. A state of wholeness can be quite easy if we are actually willing to listen to ourselves and honor what is arising.

After all: you are the empowered creator of your own life. Everything you desire comes from this place.

When we step into sovereignty, there is no need to promote our new frequency like an accolade or prize. We have less desire to judge others for what they have, for we are the creators of our inner wealth. Authentic power and self-authority don't express themselves superficially. Instead, they operate at a deep energetic level in our lives. We start to reconnect to our aliveness and this sends a resonance–a ripple effect–out into the universe. This kind of authentic power is eternal, for it relies on nothing outside of itself. It is the truest expression of your inner authority.

When we awaken, it is exactly what it sounds like: we witness ourselves fully, totally. We see what is–and what is not *yet*. That's why awakening can feel brutal: we finally start to surface the unconscious patterns that have taken over our lives. As we move through this process of learning about our choices, we start to notice something deeper underneath. Beneath all the behaviors, thoughts, and feelings lives your true being. It is this that I intend to cultivate.

Awakening isn't about the performance of wokeness. It isn't just about posting pictures of ourselves in yoga wear on the internet. For many of us, it isn't glamorous–yet those are the moments that matter most. In the end, it is about attending to the conscious practice of our lives. Awakening is rising to meet yourself in the mess because that's where most of life happens. It is about the rituals around our daily lived decisions. It is about integrating *every* aspect, even the ones we prefer not to look at. For when we walk in alignment, we are more equipped to answer the call of life.

You'll find that as you move through this book, you will start to experience changes happening in your world as you make more empowered decisions. You might have picked this book up for one reason, and you'll likely find that it illuminates much more than you initially expected. That's because awakening isn't limited to one space of our life; rather, it happens on all fronts.

My journey, in particular, has focused on the intersection of business, career, and wealth consciousness because I believe that all areas of our lives need to be attuned to our heart. We become truly successful not when we have earned the most money or acquired the most powerful title, but when we operate from an aligned place within ourselves. The work we do in the world ripples outward and is infused with our life force. It's beneficial for us to approach every part of our life with the awakened perspective, for everything is interconnected. The wealth we generate through our business and career *is* part of our spiritual work in the world. Separating them only sustains the limited perspectives that we are all trying to transcend.

Sovereignty isn't a destination, but a conversation we have with ourselves as we navigate life. After all, the practice *is* the path. The people I surround myself with express their awakening through their careers and businesses, through leadership roles and community initiatives. They are yoga teachers and film producers, writers and nutritionists, financial advisors, and real estate executives. They dream big and have bad days too. They don't know how to hold it all together, all of the time and they don't pretend to. They embody the strength of vulnerability and lead by the example they set of being real, genuine, and available for life's challenges.

Our roles, our identities, and the way we relate to others through our work in the world is being redefined. We're empowered to name our roles, our work, and our mastery. Bringing that power to bear on the world through our contributions shifts the energy and the outcomes. Something is very clear to me: the need to completely alter the way we are in relationship to our lives. As a collective, we are currently reframing the way we orient ourselves to our energetic investments: work, leisure, friendships, relationships, and partnerships. The shift is intentional because we are moving from extractive systems of consumption to expansive systems of contribution.

We have important work to do in the world and I know you're feeling it. For many of us, our career – the title, role, salary, influence, and position – largely determine our identity as we get older. This was true for me. My ego had its claws hooked into my career. And those hooks were in deep. But as I awakened and experienced more ego deaths, my attachment to my career as the definition of my success as a person has significantly shifted. I find myself asking a far more empowering question: *What's my contribution?*

We self-actualize by stepping into our life, not by perfecting it with filters and promoting it. The journey will be hard at times. That is why we gather to tell stories of our battle scars and offer our support to one another. It is vitally important to be witnessed by our trusted circle and our truth reflected to us. The challenging moments are made easier when we know we are not alone in the mess, that we will be held through our darkest moments and devastating mistakes along the way. And we will come out more alive than ever.

Your sacred task is not to let your life get lost in the noise. It is time to reattune yourself to the natural rhythm of your life. The more you can flow and use this space as a place to play on your edges; to reclaim the parts of you that feel scared and challenged, the more you will expand.

You picked up this book because you were ready. Now it's time to take the next step on your journey to sovereignty.

CHAPTER 1:

Full Body Alchemy

Mantra:

I am present. I am ready.
I am empowered.
I know who I am. I enter.

Keywords:

Alchemy, Empowerment, Initiation, Transformation,
Power, Structure, Trust

How powerful do you feel today? Take a minute and breathe into this question. Notice what it brings up in you, and how that makes you feel. There is no wrong answer to this question. The point of asking is to inquire into your beingness at this moment. How connected do you feel? How certain? How grateful? What does your inner authority look and feel like? How does it show up in your body? When was the last time you checked in with this powerful essence?

At this moment, wherever you are in your life or in your day, I invite you to take a deep breath. Allow any concepts you may hold about intuition, productivity, and transformation to melt away. Take another breath and feel into the body you inhabit. Notice where the breath travels, where it flows easily, and where it gets stuck. Then let that go too. Allow yourself to be in this moment: present to what is, without judgment, preference, or opinion. Take another breath, and settle in.

Before you enter this book fully, I want to acknowledge your commitment to your well-being and personal power. The doorway you are opening now is another crucible for your growth. There will be challenges ahead, and that is the point: when you make the decision to embrace your intrinsic power, inherent potential, and the birthright of your essential greatness, you are inevitably forced to face the parts of yourself and your life that you would rather turn away from. And almost all of us have turned away from our inner voice, inner authority, higher knowing, "spidey sense," or soul – call it whatever feels right to you because it is yours to rediscover. You are reconnecting to the Subtle.

Sometimes, maybe often or even persistently, you feel disconnected. You can't put a finger on what that is, or why you feel that way. It comes out as fatigue, exhaustion, irritability – all the issues and ailments that fall under the category of *stress*. You know that the "always-on" culture isn't serving you, but you don't know how to get off what feels like a speeding train. Perhaps stopping like just hitting the brakes – doesn't feel like an option for you. This feeling of speeding down a one-way track at uncontrollable speeds is the consequence of our current pace of culture. And to some extent, it's nearly impossible to jump ship. I think this is the reason why many people believe that they can't "get away from life" or make significant changes without disrupting everything or hurting the people around them. You don't have to. Force, fighting, and aggression have been the way – but it's only one route forward. You already know what those results look like. Thankfully, there is another way.

Walking Toward Wholeness

I'm adept at facing things head-on, crashing through a wall rather than climbing over it. Sometimes I don't notice the door that I could have opened instead. For a long time, I operated with the mindset of destroying a challenge or obstacle – anything that got in the way of my success. While that has been a reasonable solution in certain situations and has created some good in my life (and certainly plenty of funny stories), there have also been situations where that approach didn't make sense. I couldn't force the outcome in the end.

When operating in that manner, I was anchored in my "masculine" qualities; a very comfortable place for me. But a lifetime of living aggressively had left me unbalanced and disconnected from a whole other set of qualities: the "feminine" ones that I had dismissed in order to succeed. Feminine qualities such as compassion, receptivity, understanding, emotions, and flow seemed to have no place in a world dominated by masculine energies and tendencies. These energies are not rooted in gender, so it's important to know that every person has qualities of both; that's what makes us whole and complete – or imbalanced when we only access one side of our full self. It's why we must integrate every aspect of ourselves, especially the qualities that we've been told are unacceptable, ugly, or wrong. Is day better than night? Is hot better than cold? Is singing better than strategy? Is empathy weakness? Is caring counterproductive? The simple, binary answer to all those questions is: No. Your power multiplies exponentially when you accept and honor all of you – and merge all those powers within.

Many of us are used to operating in a fragmented state. This book and the practices therein serve to re-establish connection with a vital part of you: your inner authority.

Humans are incredibly adaptive. We have the ability to endure so much that we forget what it means to be whole and complete; unified within. Instead, we feel separate both inside and outside of ourselves. We don't realize, often until it is too late, that we're in the deep end of misery or a bad deal. Then, with bewilderment, we wonder: What did I miss? What went wrong? Disappointment or rage overtake us: How did that happen? Why didn't it work out? And all too often, we turn on ourselves: What is wrong with me? *Why didn't I see it coming?* Perhaps we're not asking ourselves the right questions.

We are working against ourselves by battling something within us that we've defined as a problem. Many of us live in cultures that condition us to approach our issues with harsh tactics that promise to get rid of our discomfort rather than tend to the issue itself. This inner war we wage on ourselves in search of the picture-perfect life weighs heavily on our internal resources. It depletes our energy and makes it harder to see the opportunities life is presenting to us in order to illuminate the path to self-mastery. We resist, deny, and try to force an outcome that simply wasn't meant to be. Trust in the unknown? The unseen is tantamount to lunacy. The "unproven" is exiled and othered: intuition isn't measurable, productivity is. Surrendering control to a "higher power" is akin to death – just ask your ego.

The Power of the Present Moment

This path offers many lessons, often hard ones that send us into spirals of self-doubt, recrimination, and judgment. When we've always done things one way and believed it was the only way, it can be hard to accept that we had, in fact, been betraying ourselves. But don't stay there for long! When you begin to wake up to the sheer power of your insights, subtle faculties, and intuitive skills, you won't want to spend much time ruminating over the past or what could have been. There is so much to look into *presently.*

Take a minute and reflect on how you're showing up today. What is here with you? Notice which beliefs and ideas are operating under the surface. Do you feel excited and energized by what you might discover on your quest for intuitive integration and self-mastery? Or are you nervous to dig into the work here because it might reveal something that you're not ready to work with yet? Maybe your mind is skeptical, and your ego is acting up: resisting, denying, deprecating, and generally trying to distract you with fear and complacency. Do you feel worthy of your big vision? Do you feel ready for your success? Whatever your current mood or state of mind and body, take a minute to notice your feelings, thoughts, and energy levels. It is important to acknowledge where your baseline is in this moment, so you can more clearly map your intuitive trajectory as you interact with the exploratory invitations in this book.

I present these invitations as reflections, self-inquiry, and actionable practices. This is our *inner work*. I use the word work because getting aligned with our intuitive nature is not a passive exercise. It's very active, but it's not "work" in the way we may normally think of it. This work is like shaping a stone to find the sculpture within it. You're not in the quarry, you're in the studio. So, approach your inner work with reverence. We'll chip away at the things that have been holding you back from accessing your subtle faculties. We'll activate your transcendent intelligence centers. You'll anchor into your inner authority – that unique, authentic essence that speaks only to you and for you. Then, the onus of action is on you to be the agent of transformation.

The simple foundation of our Inner Work is *awareness*. Noticing without judgment; with the curiosity of a child that observes every new thing with awe. How you feel today, right now, is exactly as it should be. The transformation always begins when we acknowledge what's real for us in *every* moment. You'll start to notice a shift as you integrate aspects of yourself you didn't know you had, or those you have hidden away, ignored, or outright rejected. You'll notice life becomes more responsive to *you.*

In a post-COVID World, we're addressing the emergence of, and opportunity to build, new structures to support our inner and outer worlds. External forces have put us face-to-face with fears we didn't know we had – along with dreams and desires we forgot long ago. This is a forced dismantling of the old systems. More than ever, we must trust ourselves.

More than at any time in human history, we are able to access and embody all of who we are. There is no holding back. There is no playing small any longer. We have the knowledge we need at our fingertips. In a world of awakened leaders, nobody needs to overpower or control anyone. We can all be free simply by rising to live responsibly on behalf of All.

Your potential is in the present moment, which requires discipline and devotion to the process of becoming exactly who you are. Most of us hide in some form because living at this level can feel uncomfortable at first. It demands that we step into life with our total power and authority. Usually, this surfaces some inconvenient and often painful truths about the choices we've made out of fear. All of this is the last thing you want to do because it goes against every single thing you've been told will help you succeed.

The Joy of Self-Discovery

Your sovereignty and sense of well-being rest in your own hands. It lives in your willingness to self-inquire, self-reflect, and to sit with yourself in deep honesty.

Your "best life" is not something that exists in the future outside of you; it emerges from your willingness to be present with things now. By being completely connected to your body, willing to feel all your emotions, and unravel the gnarliest patterns, you start to realize the power you have to make subtle, yet profound shifts. *You are personally responsible for rising above the conditioning you grew up with.*

My goal is to empower you to find both strength and joy in the deep work of self-discovery. You are making yourself whole by the power of your intention, inquiry, and integration. By the end of this book, I hope you crave new challenges, because now you are fully accessing your subtle powers, feelers, signals, and intelligence. You are empowered by the knowledge that each issue you face is an invaluable tool that will unlock more of your latent inner strengths and hidden gifts. I want to embolden you to actively seek out the places in you that feel weak or undeveloped and make a commitment to strengthen them with tender love, attention, and compassion.

This book is not here to pound you with more ways to eliminate your problems because the reality is: life will continue to deliver more "problems." We can't escape them nor erase them. Instead, we work *with* them, reframe them, and learn from them; they are ingredients in our personal alchemy. Alas, it turns out that our problems are not in our way; our problems *are* the way.

I wrote this book for anyone who has held back from their true nature; who has held it in and held it together. I'm writing for the woman and the man who want to know that embodying the fullness of who you are is worth it, even if it doesn't feel comfortable at first. This book is a friend, a trusted resource, and a guide for you as you embark on the path to embodied self-mastery; a warrior's path. Warriors honor their hearts first and the connection to the infallible wisdom that guides their actions. This has been my path as well. I show up for you in my sovereignty, embodied through my transformational process. I unraveled all that I thought I was so that I could know the truth of who I AM.

The Trappings of the Transformation Economy

Consumers are spending more money than ever on products and services that promise to soothe the ache of our increasingly chaotic lives or optimize our potential – from upgraded coffee beans, on-demand yoga, and smart wearables to personalized retreats. We watch inspirational videos over lunch, meditate with apps, talk to our plants, go to therapy, and hire a business coach. Our drive to optimize has driven the Health & Wellness industry to $4.2 trillion globally in just a few years. We are high-performance beings who are actively seeking powerful ways to improve our experience of life. After all: the goal of life is to become more conscious, not less.

The transformation economy, as defined by economists Joseph Pine and James H. Gilmore, is predicated on one simple principle: the product is *You*. Your will to improve, optimize, ascend, or simply feel better is a human prerogative. From the Vedas to Maslow, we have understood for centuries that humans seek self-actualization as a matter of evolutionary impulse. However, we are increasingly looking for help externally while simultaneously handing over our self-actualization – often to companies whose only prerogative is to keep us in the funnel and cross-sell at every data-driven interaction. Ask yourself: is the transformation you want to achieve aligned with the transformation *they* want you to achieve?

Behind the movement to care for ourselves better in a world that feels more fragmented than ever is a dark trend that keeps people disempowered. The persistent emphasis on "finding solutions" for our problematized lives leads us to believe that we are broken or that we are not reaching our potential. We're led to believe that we aren't doing enough – and by proxy, that we aren't enough. Who wants to feel like they are ineffective or mediocre? Not me! Who feels like they have to prove that they aren't wasting time or opportunities? Also me!

More concerning, we develop an unconscious expectation that our challenges can be managed by consuming more things: more products, more videos, more experiences. We add knowledge, courses, books, equipment, supplements, routines, and rituals to our busy days. In trying to attend to our healing, we ironically end up feeding our addictions and distractions. In trying to be more productive and effective, we add more To Do lists to our crowded desktops and calendars. We're no longer able to trust our abilities because we've outsourced all solutions. Then we wonder why nothing works for long.

To be clear, I'm not saying we shouldn't avail ourselves of any of this. I am a consumer: I have a library of personal development books, a collection of crystals, and a well-stocked supplements shelf; I have a morning ritual, a beauty ritual, and a contemplative practice; I work with trainers, therapists, and shamans. One of the most poignant lessons I've learned in my self-actualization is that I don't need any of the above. We cannot rely on tools; we must rely on ourselves.

We tend to think of transformation as a process by which we stop being who we are to become someone else, whether that's the authentic self or a better self. I've come to understand that no matter how much I wake up, let go, or release, I'm still me. I'm different, but also fundamentally still the same person at the end of the day. We don't transform into an alter-ego or unrecognizable bot. That's not the point! Why would you be born if you weren't supposed to be you? What transformation does is help us drop the artificial masks and crutches we've relied on to carry us when we feel scared or weak. We drop the habits, defense-mechanisms, beliefs, and patterns that we unconsciously identified with to become who we are. So, what's really happening is that you're learning to dis-identify while you dis-cover what's beneath: the you that you've always wanted to connect with and embody. Whether that's a stronger you, a better you, or a more handsome you doesn't matter. You are all of that already. The threshold to knowing that truth is to accept who you are in this exact moment and, perhaps paradoxically, who you have been in the past. Your acceptance of the person – and the patterns – that have brought you here serve your self-actualization as much as daily meditation or yoga does. When you feel better about being who you are, you move into a space of self-acceptance and self-love. That is the space that facilitates transformation and self-actualization.

I'd like to make a suggestion for those who don't naturally equate profession with personal transformation: what if your job, vocation, or career are transformative? Think about this for a minute. Have you changed, grown, and evolved through professional experiences? What if you could approach your work as a vehicle for self-actualization? If a brand can sell transformation, then a person can engage their work in a transformative experience, by choice. Leading others or building teams is the transformation economy. Entrepreneurship is the transformation economy! You evolve at light-speed when you take on a new role, challenge, or go all-in with an entrepreneurial route. With a shift in perception, you can view just about anything, including your job, as transformational - because everything is an opportunity to express your highest potential - and that is the essence of transformation.

Letting Go of the Illusion

When you start to align with your inner authority, your old world will fall apart. This can look an infinite number of ways, but the core truth is this: what no longer resonates will fall away. Your ideas of safety and security might change. You might feel helpless or resistant to what's happening because it is terrifying to watch your world change to fit your new shape. You might try and hold it together at first, looking for new ways to control your environment or strategize a familiar solution. But these are band-aids that will temporarily mask the fact that you have changed. It's like trying to wear your childhood clothes as an adult: they are worn out, too small, and out of style.

I don't say all this to scare you. I share this truth because it is a fundamental fact of the catharsis process, which is what you will go through if you are dedicated to aligning yourself with your inner authority. We are given opportunities to evolve when a defining moment destroys the fabric of our reality as we knew it and shows us something unexpected or unknown about ourselves.

Letting go of the psychological safety net that supports your reality can look and feel destructive – and it is. Think of a mighty oak tree. Before the tree took on its final form, it had to survive as a small acorn. It weathered droughts, wildfires, and devastating rains. It grew through storms and pestilence. The small seed had to push through heavy earth first, and it kept on growing and going for years after that. But before all that could happen, the seed had to make the choice to crack open its protective shell and face the elements that would ultimately help it become resilient. Oaks are strong because they've weathered so much. Your destiny is no different; you're not meant to stay small inside the protective safety of your conditioning.

The paradox is: to grow big, you must endure many small deaths. This is why *Dune* author Frank Herbert referred to fear as the "little-death" – when we can confront our fears, we face our core fear of death and transcend. Fear comes from limitation and scarcity; a sense of lack. If we believe we will *only* be loved a certain way or that there is only one particular path to success, then we have limited ourselves and increased our suffering. The caterpillar must die to become the butterfly, and once we outgrow our old self, there's no stopping the process of metamorphosis. You can resist (we all do at first) or you can work with the energy and intuition that's already cultivating the new you.

The lesson every great teaching has for humans: as much as we might try, we cannot control the universe. You can only control your response. Life is a great teacher in this process. The sooner you acknowledge that you can't control the situation, the sooner you can enter into a more empowered process: directing your inner authority through conscious choice.

I've navigated major life changes and massive obstacles because I never stopped seeking my truth. I didn't rest at what some expert said, especially when I could find as many counter-arguments and experts saying the opposite. I've endured undiagnosed depression, eating disorders, and other mental illnesses. I've committed "career suicide" and experienced burn out in my professional world. I've put myself out there and experienced trolling at the hands of strangers. I've wondered what life was all about, and whether it was worth it. But I never let any of that stop me, at least not for long.

The Resilient Essence

I believe resilience is the byproduct of overcoming fears and transcending limitations, whether internal or external. I have come to understand that on the other side of fear is truth. And we have to work for it because we're wired to be afraid of fear and its mini-me: discomfort. I've been crippled by heartbreak and then I transformed my pain into my power. Over, and over, and over again. I know how insurmountable the challenges can seem in the moment. I've questioned my choices. Yet no amount of chasing solutions or pretending to "have it all together" in order to feel validated by someone else's opinion made any of the hard times better–or easier. In the end, we are here to grow through the struggle, for it forges us to be stronger, clearer, more decisive–and more powerful. We make better decisions after we confront what's in front of us and learn the necessary lessons. We make empowered choices when we feel whole, complete, and connected to our intrinsic power.

Even though I hurt a lot at times, in the end, I always landed on yes. Yes, my truth is worth it. Yes, I am worth it. The ugly feelings come and go, and thus can't be "it." Along the way, I gained strength and resolved to keep going. I developed an unshakable belief in myself as I navigated my transformational journey or "awakening." It asked of me more than I thought I could give, courage I didn't know I had, and faith I didn't know I had lost. As Carl Jung famously stated, "Until you make the unconscious conscious, it will direct your life and you will call it fate."

So, I doubled down on waking up and stepped into what I deeply desired without holding back my authentic essence. I decided I was done trying to limit myself to one definition. I'm a businesswoman and an executive – and I'm also a student of the mystical arts. I train leaders on how to unlock their visionary capacity and make more effective decisions – and I also hold sacred circles in my home. I speak regularly at conferences and have run successful teams in male-dominated industries – and I talk about "soft" stuff like the heart's intelligence. There are many facets to me, and I like it that way! My professional pursuits are only one aspect of my expertise. The interests, investments, and investigations that feed me span the spectrum. I have spent years studying everything from neuroscience and quantum physics to psychology and shamanism, nutrition and fitness to energy healing and philosophy, mystic traditions, spirituality, and ancient cultures. And I still love my real estate deals, investing, economics, and personal finance.

I've had readers of my newsletter write me angry emails when I talked about the importance of money. I've had random people tell me I'm worthless because I dared to leave my first husband when I finally admitted that the relationship was bringing me down instead of building me up. I've had friends leave because I started standing up for myself and what I believed in. I've had business partners forsake the equity I earned in companies I helped to build. I've had people tell me not to try something new, not to take an unproven approach or tell me that I can't show up in the world as I am - because it scares *them*. But it doesn't scare me. No, my inner authority directs and empowers me.

The more I've stepped into my power the more resources, support, and collaborators have shown up to meet me where I am. I met my soulmate, Andrew, a year after I left my first marriage. As an entrepreneur, I've given myself the freedom to explore more of my interests and experiment with my path. I've had the opportunity to work with major corporate clients and partners around the world, building notable brands and inspiring products. I've helped to launch people's start-ups, careers, and dreams. I've been invited to share my story multiple times on stage and each time I've gone deeper I've had more of me welcomed and received. I've been supported by my community in some of my darkest periods of grief, pain, and frustration. No, none of this has been easy–but it's all been worth it.

Although it took some time for me to bring my whole self to the table, I now show up with more power at my disposal. The haters show me *their* edge. They invite me to shine brighter. I went through years of burnout and breakdown before I finally went within for the answers I was seeking outside of me. No amount of external knowledge could replace what I learned when I did the inner work. When I finally came back to my body and welcomed all of me in, I unlocked parts of myself I thought I had thrown away forever. I started to love myself for the first time. I became responsible for and accountable to every single part of my life, especially the parts I had tried so hard to hide from everyone else – including myself.

Both / And

It was here that I learned the important lesson about the split that humans create within themselves: this idea that things are either/or. That we are either rational or emotional, intelligent or intuitive, productive or inert (unmotivated), active or passive – that we are either one thing or the other, whatever that may be. Yet the either/or paradigm is a fallacy. Humans are Both/ And. We are both rational *and* emotional, intellectual *and* instinctive, intelligent *and* intuitive, loving *and* fierce, professional *and* playful. We're supposed to explore, expand, and evolve.

The path to our greatest power isn't a joyride. Claiming your authority isn't an easy fix – it's the only way to sovereignty. Self-responsibility through radical self-acceptance and self-love is the key that unlocks the door to your inner authority: the power you came here to claim. It's my hope I can help you to avoid some of the common traps that keep you stuck and in resistance to going exactly where you need to be.

Throughout this book, I will share pieces of my story in order to illuminate the wisdom I've integrated as a result of moving past pain and discomfort, listening to my intuition, and evolving through defining moments. Wisdom comes from experience, not from mental concepts or philosophy alone. When we've lived through something, we gain credibility because we have wisdom to share with others. When we share our stories as a vehicle for transmitting higher wisdom, we become facilitators of awakening and growth.

Finally, may I remind you that there is no guru. You are the answer you've been seeking. All you desire begins within you. Once that sinks in and becomes your guiding truth, you will be unstoppable. This is the first and most foundational truth I want you to reflect upon today: that the only thing standing in the way of your most powerful life is *you*.

Reflection Questions:

1. Who am I without all my roles, masks, and identities?

   ____

   ____

   ____

   ____

2. What does my true essence look, smell, taste, hear, feel, and act like when no one else is influencing me?

   ____

   ____

   ____

   ____

3. What is something I diminish or minimize to make others around me feel safe? What can I reclaim about myself that got lost?

   ____

   ____

   ____

   ____

Actionable Practices:

1. Take stock of your world. Who are you? List out your beliefs, roles, identities, expectations, and obligations to people or things external to you.

   ____

   ____

   ____

   ____

   a. When you are done, notice how YOU are bigger than all of these ideas you hold about who you are. You are not your story, your job, your history, or your memories. You are a process, unfolding.

   ____

   ____

   ____

   ____

2. Using the list above, circle the instances where you feel that you are "either/or".

   a. Write out the pairs that conflict. For example, I am either strong or vulnerable; I must be either a parent or a friend.

   ____

   ____

   ____

   ____

b. Feel into that experience of either/or. What does it feel like?

____

____

____

____

c. Now, try re-framing using Both/And.

____

____

____

____

d. Review your list carefully, and notice if anything shifts internally. Can you accept that you are Both/And? How does that feel?

____

____

____

____

3. Practice of presence. Throughout the day, try to remind yourself to be present. Notice, stop, and pay detailed attention to the moment. Whatever you are doing, do it with intention. Notice how you feel about your surroundings: the colors, smells, and movements. Notice how things feel to the touch and how your body feels. Notice what is going on around you. Even if you practice for just a minute, you can

experience profound results in your overall sense of stability and wellbeing.

Go Deeper:

1. *The Transformation Economy* by Joseph Pine and James H. Gilmore

2. *Maslow's Hierarchy of Needs* by Abraham Maslow

3. *The Vedas* by Various Authors

CHAPTER 2

Productive Intuition

Mantra:

I give myself permission to exist, to be here,

to want more for myself.

I accept my intuitive nature.

I redefine reality to serve my highest potential.

Keywords:

Stillness, Space, Simplicity, Self-Connection,

Productivity, Intuition

When I talk about productive intuition, what do I really mean? In a world that deeply equates success with externalized production of economic value, it's important to slow down and clarify the meaning behind each word. Before I do that, I ask you to reflect on your personal definitions. What does "productive" bring up for you? What is your relationship with the word "intuition"?

Our culture often associates productivity with time-based activities: how much did we do today? What was our output? We are told we have to get enough done, and then some more. We feel we are not worthy if we don't fill every minute with something to do. Being busy is mistaken for productivity. We invest in apps and planners that promise to help us organize our to-do lists, but are we becoming any more efficient? Is it in service to our true nature to define productivity in quantitative terms? We trade time for money, but it never feels like we have enough of either. Where do our dreams fit into this equation? Is there room for our desires or do we only have enough to survive? Do we want our sacred time each day to be spent counting the number of steps that lay between us and our elusive, fleeting concepts of success? If you're anything like me, you are probably finding that this idea of productivity has been limiting your reach, your dreams, and your potential.

Sometimes, the friction we experience in our lives is a result of our unconscious definitions and stories. We can reject concepts that don't fit with our worldview, or that feel too fluffy, woo, or ungrounded. This was how I felt about any concept that claimed to be "heart-centered" for a long time. I was all about business and it wasn't until I started connecting to my heart that I was able to shift my original definition to be much more expansive. This process changed my life because I was able to open myself up to new experiences, practices, and powerful habits that supported my growth. But first – I had to move past my original assumptions.

It's time to align to a more productive definition of productivity. What would you like that to be? Redefining words and refining the language you use every day is a subtle shift that generates massive impact. Do you know how much power you hold over your experience simply by carefully selecting the words you use? Words provide meaning, and occasionally we accept these definitions or ideas without questioning them. Yet if you look back on your life, you'll notice that your language has evolved as you changed. The meaning of the words we use evolves without our conscious awareness or participation. And those words – the language you use to describe your reality – often become stories before we realize it. Those stories become beliefs, and those beliefs drive behaviors. What results are you getting?

It's time to notice the words you use regularly and take that a step further. Ask yourself: what meaning have I assigned to these words? What language am I choosing to use here? Don't be afraid to challenge your own definitions. Only then will you see where they have limited you.

Words can only take us so far. Speech, like the ego, is limited; both restrict our experience of reality. Labels are narrow experientially, yet become powerful barriers between what is meant to be experienced and a corresponding word. When I look at different languages, especially languages based on pictorial representations, like Chinese or Japanese, or even Egyptian hieroglyphs, I see that pictures or images are far more expansive. They tell stories and within that are numerous interpretations. You can better understand the nuances that are communicated within them; subtly sensed. Numbers are also language, geometry is a language, math is a language, music is a language, art is a language, movement is a language. We have the ability to communicate in so many ways – why use just one?

Our intuition operates in the same way: we have multiple sensory languages that convey important information to us. To emphasize one form of intellect at the expense of all others diminishes your ability to harness all your embodied wisdom. Intuition is both a language and wisdom beyond language. I think of this as "transcendent intelligence."

Humans are transmitter-receivers for multiple forms of transcendent intelligence, which we access through our subtle faculties and intuition. The brain is brilliant and necessary; a super-computer that processes better than anything humans have invented. But here's the thing: brilliant ideas aren't generated by the mind alone. They become more accessible when you connect to a greater source of wisdom: your total truth. But in order to cultivate this ability, you have to be genuinely curious.

Can you recall a time when you had a full-blown, fully formed understanding of a big, complex idea or thought? Maybe you "just knew," or you "saw the path" forward. Maybe you even "saw the future" in the form of a clear vision or embodied understanding. How many times have you dismissed a knowing or flash of genius as "too crazy" only to find out later that someone else created the thing you envisioned?

Carl Jung, one of the pre-eminent psychologists of all time, posited that we are all connected through what he called the collective unconscious: a wellspring of every human thought, idea, and impulse beneath the surface of our conscious awareness. Quantum physicists have proven that everything, including me and you, is electromagnetic in nature. We are not physical beings but rather pure energy taking form. In other words, while we might have a physical body, we are still connected to, and in constant communication with, unseen, subtle, powerful forces. We are all tapped into the same source of infinite, generative creativity. Some call it the Luminous Matrix, others Divine Source. Quantum physicists would refer to this as the Unified Field.

Many of us already realize we are innately powerful, we just need the tools to help us turn on the tap. In examining my relationship to the word "productivity" I realized that the energy of the word is generative: it is about expressing our desire to create. This generative, creative essence is what connects definitions of productivity, yet this one feels far more embracing and expansive of possibility.

For example, I used to believe creativity was only the domain of artists. For most of my life, I didn't consider myself a creative person because I was good at "regular" school and received accolades, acceptance, and validation for that accomplishment. Besides, my sister claimed the identity of the artist in our family as her drawing skills were quite evident when she was only 4 years old. I took on the role of the "smart one" and strove to excel at school, and pursued a career in banking, financial planning, and in the last decade, as an entrepreneur in tech-enabled investing and real estate syndication. I brushed aside my love of writing poetry. I didn't carve out space to cultivate my other artistic skills and abilities because I believed that my academic intelligent side would better serve me in life – and to some extent, it has. Yet it wasn't until I claimed these creative, vulnerable parts of me that I could show up fully as my whole self, and embody my inner authority.

We've over-invested in the primacy of intellect while dismissing our primal intuitive nature. Your true source of infinite generativity lives in your heart – the home of the divine artist in us all. The ego likes to think it has the best ideas and inventions, but the truth is that we are downloading this information from the infinite quantum field. This might come as a shock to those who are identified with their Achiever – the one who produces things that create value. Most of us who are embedded in some form of capitalism have been conditioned to identify with our ability to produce according to externally accepted standards. Yet I invite you to try on an expanded perspective: if you are not attached to one identity, then you are not limited by it.

The 'Myth' of Productivity

When we live with the story that productivity is intrinsic to our worth and value in the outside world, it becomes easy to equate success with staying busy and focusing on the "doing" of things to guarantee our rank. Yet this idea injures us. It makes us more invested in other people's versions of success, rather than in cultivating trust in our creative genius.

Real productivity feels counter-intuitive to the traditional definition. For, in order to give ourselves over to the process of creation, we must enter the space of "no-mind" – the impulse that drives us to put pen to paper, paint to canvas, words to music. We must enter a space of sacred trust with our mysterious muse, the creatrix that waits for us to silence the mind so it can speak. The paradox here is that the more we slow down and learn to quiet the mind from all the external chatter, the easier it is for the real clarity to come through. In other words: it is *less* action and *more* being that frees our genius.

With a little research, we find that throughout all of history, the greatest thinkers, scientists, and inventors all carve out time and space to be in the "no-mind" zone; where ideas and inspiration flow in, and divine intelligence works through us. Many great Western minds such as Einstein, Tesla, Edison, Newton, and Darwin were known to be notorious wanders, tinkerers, and putterers who made time each day to create from a place of inspired contemplation. Even though the pace of innovation has picked up since the industrial revolution turned into the information revolution, the nature of what drives innovation hasn't changed. Ultra-successful pioneers like the late Steve Jobs and Warren Buffett prioritize their creative productivity by '"taking" time and making space to practice stillness, meditation, and contemplation.

The classic definition of productivity usually fixates on output: the tangible, "proven" results that demonstrate our efforts were "worth it." This linear equation mentality is dangerous, for it fundamentally values human beings as cogs in the economic machine rather than the multi-dimensional beings we are. When we strive to fit our infinite potential into this tiny box, we exhaust ourselves from trying to stay so small all the time. It becomes a constant striving, a force that seems to control us rather than unleash our natural vitality. It creates a momentum that feels unnatural and overwhelming – because it is. This momentum is not sustainable.

We crave to release ourselves from this unsustainable pace, and yet at the same time, we fear the silence, the pause. The full stop. Anyone who meditates is familiar with the terror that can arise in the no-mind place. But in trying to avoid it, we fuel our burnout. How beautiful that eventually, inevitably, we are returned to the place we were trying to escape in the first place. This is why meditation seems so simple on the surface –sit in place –and yet profoundly powerful in the capacity it builds internally.

Silence is the Clearest Mirror

Silence is the clearest mirror. In this space, all we can do is witness ourselves – and at times, our struggle. Boredom is a symptom of our desire to disengage from the world. If you feel that silence is boring, you might be afraid. In today's world, it is easier to be entertained than engaged. It is easier to consume than create. Boredom happens when we "turn off" rather than attune our relationship with the world around us.

The truth is, silence is an active space. It creates magnetism in our energy field, pulling forward the information and downloads we need to bring forth our best work. In the contemplation of our vision, we can imagine all possibilities. In the potentiated space of our imagination, we can give voice and form to our wildest dreams and ideas. Here, you plant the conscious seeds of your future success, and here, in the silence, you tend to them. The silence supports you in learning where your authentic inner authority lives.

If you are reading this book, perhaps it's because at some point you too grew tired of being inside the machine. Maybe you got burned out. Perhaps you couldn't name the tension exactly, but you knew that a way of doing things wasn't working. Even though part of you was afraid of things changing, a bigger part knew they could no longer stay the same. And that part of you is what got you here.

I put so much emphasis on the definition of productivity because it's an important distinction to make when defining how we embody and bring forth value. You are not here to lose yourself again in the same life-sucking systems of overconsumption and overproduction. You are here to bring forth life-giving ideas and innovations that serve the world, regardless of what your "role" looks like.

We cultivate our centeredness not by committing to a million different things that make us feel important, but in bringing our energy inward, back into our center. Where you are better able to attune and hear the voice of your authentic inner authority give clear directions for how to honor your whole self, not just your Achiever. When we focus on cultivating our essence rather than chasing success, you are able to do more with less.

Inner silence is where the real work begins. If you feel like life has gotten too loud, it's time to gather yourself in and take a moment to pause. Productivity isn't mindless busyness. Productivity is rooted generativity. Being able to hold space for yourself is the definition of powerful, for it is here that you become power-filled. If you can't generate the lifeforce for yourself first, how will you sustain your future success?

Thus, prioritizing and holding the space to meet yourself first is of the utmost necessity. Many people I know struggle to carve out time for themselves, myself included. We all have demands on our time and so we must discern between urgency and importance. There are urgent things to attend to every day – but are they important? If you are not centered in yourself and your inner authority, it's hard to know what is important. Cultivating your center is akin to developing a martial arts mindset: your composure and access to your inner knowing give you more clarity in the moment to choose the most impactful action. When you are connected to your inner authority, you claim your decisions with confidence and conviction. You move forward with trust in your vision. You take action and develop the ability to respond to a multitude of situations that strengthen you and your gifts. You become more capable and you build capacity to handle more complexity. Your ability to hold your center in the face of challenges trains you to meet the external chaos with more ingenuity and resilience.

Knowing Your Potential

We've talked about the productive part of Productive Intuition. Now it's time to touch on the intuition piece and how to use intuition to move potential into conscious productivity. The reasoning mind loves facts, so it's important to get the left brain onboard with the integration of your intuition. The linear way of thinking that many of us are enculturated in wants to see validation, proof, tested methods; a recipe that can be guaranteed. Our rational mind prefers this way of approaching a solution because it's less risky. Two-thirds of the electrical activity in the brain is related to vision, so it's no wonder we think we need to see something to believe it, and mistrust the "invisible" instinct. As humans, we are wired to minimize our exposure to risk, even as we reach for the heavens. We're a frustrating paradox, aren't we?

Here's the thing: intuition isn't just a feeling – it's a *knowing*. In fact, Google defines it as our ability to understand something *without* additional reasoning. Intuition is the body's knowing before the mind's reasoning comes online. Our brain is just one part of our toolkit that helps us "make sense" of things, whereas your intuition emerges from an embodied experience of all the body's data-gathering devices. It's one of our most ancient sense-making centers. Because intuition isn't linear and doesn't function in the same way for everybody, it's gotten a bad rap as "wishy-washy" or "woo." In traditionally masculine spaces – for many of us, that's our professional environments – intuition isn't respected as a valuable source of wisdom, for it's not based on straightforward facts.

Intuition is generally categorized as "feminine" as compared to the intellect, which is decidedly masculine. Intuition, like almost all feminine traits and qualities, was historically persecuted and reviled as evil, inferior, and occasionally a good reason for death. Intuition, Emotions, Nature, Cycles all went against the rules of "Man." Yet this form of external control is losing its hold. We're *supposed* to work with our intuition. It is as natural to humans as breathing – and just like breathing, we hardly ever give it a second thought.

Intuition can surface in many ways, depending on how your body speaks to you. It might feel like tingles or a clenched stomach, an ah-ha breakthrough or a subtle whisper. However it surfaces, it's your inner authority trying to speak to you, help you, and guide you.

Usually, our inner authority comes through to get our attention and show us a way that is more easeful and graceful than one we've been trying. The ego loves to be the hero; it recruits the mind to create strategies and solutions that harness your skills. But the ego is not a source of wisdom and can often mislead us. In other words, your mind serves your innate heart wisdom and not the other way around. While our mind's logic might make more "sense" on the surface, your inner authority speaks the language of your subtle, intuitive faculties. We do not prioritize this language in Western cultures, and so we must learn to cultivate it on our own. Your intuition's language might not make sense at first, so learning to trust in your inner authority when it speaks is imperative to the work ahead.

Learning to Listen

Allowing life to work through us requires some surrender of our reasoning. It does not ask us to surrender ourselves (only ego asks that of us) but rather surrender our need to *control* the situation. Our trust in the serendipity of life builds other, subtle skills that will serve us better than a false sense of control over our fluctuating world. The more you cultivate spaces of silence in your being and in your life, the easier it will be to drop into your center. The more you cultivate your center, the more resilient you become in the face of challenges because you know your truth.

When you're able to respond instead of react, you can more clearly see what life is presenting you with in the moment, and make more conscious decisions that serve you and the world. When you are able to see the lesson or gift of the moment, you are aligning yourself with the transcendent intelligence that permeates and guides our lives from inside. This transcendent intelligence is part of the genius that comes through you in moments of inspired creativity and clear thinking. This genius cycles throughout the collective and renews itself, others, and you endlessly. The real miracle happens when we get out of the way and allow this inspired genius to guide our inner authority towards the creative solutions that break the constraints of limiting beliefs and behaviors.

Learning how to decode the intelligence and inspiration we receive is part of the trust-building process. For example, you might feel a subtle impulse or experience an unexpected thought. Sometimes this feels like instructions to pull over, stop what we're doing, switch directions, or try a new way of doing something. These thoughts can feel inconvenient– maybe you don't have the time to entertain it or the original thought doesn't make sense. Perhaps it feels like a diversion or distraction. Perhaps you aren't "that kind of person." Most of the time, we don't know exactly what it means – and so we brush it off as silly.

Yet when we dismiss our inner voice without considering it as a source of embodied information, we break trust with ourselves. We affirm our limitations. We say no to serendipity. We are conditioned to think that working more means that we've done more or are worth more, but life doesn't follow this equation. Life presents us with opportunities to expand us, because life is generative by nature. To honor the impulse is to allow the multi-dimensional knowledge of your being to speak. In doing so, we are shown something miraculous – a fortuitous encounter, a chance meeting, a required item we've been seeking, or a piece of information that can make all the difference in our world. In a non-linear universe, there's no limit to what can happen.

When you tap into the embodied knowing of your inner authority, you access your intuition. The more you listen to and allow yourself to be fully expressed in your knowing, the more empowered you will become. Ultimately, inner authority is rooted in and rests on a deep self-acceptance of all that we are. With this connection, we stop aiming for perfection for we don't seek to be anything but *exactly what we already are.* There is less conflict in our field about what's truly right for us versus what might be expected of us by others in our life, for we have a connection to the intelligence that permeates everything.

Truth isn't a fixed place with one definition, it's a form of inner perception. We clarify our perception the more we connect with our inner authority and learn how to listen to its wisdom. It can be challenging to discern truth when there's so much noise in the world. We are all surrounded by news sources that claim to know what's happening, but no one holds the whole truth we are seeking – because it's not outside of us. It's inside your being. Being in touch with our intuition helps us discern between helpful information and hurtful information. It strengthens your sovereignty so you are not so easily manipulated by headlines or influencers or ad-driven media sites.

The Power of Our Defining Moments

I write this book in a post-pandemic world, where we are in the beginning stages of a massive restructuring of life on Earth as we know it. It is still too early to know with any accuracy what comes next, but a few imperatives have been clear for a long time. We are being asked to create more regenerative systems and structures, both internally and externally. Faced with a situation that has no solution in sight, humanity must contend with its precarious situation.

Life will always present us with situations that are meant to "break us" open. If you are invested in developing yourself, unconsciously you will call forward the challenges that will test you, because this is how life strengthens you. This is not to diminish the very real experience of millions of people around the world who have been impacted by COVID-19. No one who got sick "deserved" this. Rather, I think it's important to not lose sight of the larger picture unfolding: an invisible virus can upend hundred-year-old systems in a matter of weeks. Something smaller than a dot of ink has reshaped reality as we now know it.

Moments that break us open are extremely uncomfortable – they are not designed to be easy for how else would they bring forward our true courage and grit? How else would we cultivate our resilience and creativity if we didn't experience constraints? Growth doesn't always feel good. The truth is, the medicine we need is usually quite different than what we would normally invite into our life. And that's the point. We don't get to control the process of our evolution. We don't get to say when and where transformation will show up to shift our trajectory. Life chooses for us. The only thing we get to choose is how we show up.

Through our challenges, we gain the tools and skills that we'll need for the next part of our journey. We are exposed to the places inside us that need development and attention: our wounds. We also get to bear witness to our strength and truth. Challenges are essential, even if they are not always welcome friends on the journey. They remove what's no longer working so we can move forward. These moments can be profoundly liberating if we are willing to turn and face them; to feel them fully.

Often, our challenges become our defining moments. *Lightning moments*: when we are struck by an invisible force that forever alters the course of our lives. The battles we face and the mistakes we make along the way teach us how to embody our true self by showing us what *is* the path and what is not. What doesn't serve us doesn't come with us in the next chapter of the journey. Take a minute and survey your life: what were some of your defining moments– and why? What choice were you presented with? What made this moment significant in the larger arc of your life story?

Every powerful transformational process has a teaching for you. Sometimes, it will help you see important challenges and constraints; other times more subtle aspects will be revealed. Sometimes you won't know right away. The mind can't always conceptualize the powerful lessons that impact us in a myriad of ways, because in the end, this is heart-based work. Yet each one of us is capable of quantum leaps if we are willing to receive and integrate the lessons of our deepest challenges. It turns out that if we do the work, we become capable of miracles.

Wisdom is a Process of Subtraction

It's easy to add up the data of our lives and think we know what it all means, but oftentimes this is where we get lost instead. Wisdom does emerge over time, but it's not how much we've learned that counts – it's what we've done with it. Ironically enough, it's often when we let go of what we used to believe that our actual wisdom shows up. Wisdom is a process of subtraction.

This runs against the standard idea of wisdom as accretive: more age, more lessons, more experiences. All this equates to expertise, we might reason. But you can go through life having millions of experiences and learn nothing of value about yourself. You can age but never grow up; never gain any wisdom at all. It's not the things in and of themselves that provide wisdom but rather the kernel of insight we extract and apply to our life to improve upon it. When we reflect on what our insights, lessons, and takeaways are as a result of our experience, we are able to effectively resource ourselves with the teachings of these rich encounters. It is *this* well that we call wisdom.

We don't get to truth by adding more, we get to truth by stripping away the decoration and seeing what remains. What does this look like in reality? When it comes to connecting to our inner authority, the thing we need to subtract the most is the mental processes that dominate our intuitive abilities. How many times have you dismissed a thought or an idea because it felt risky? Because it didn't jibe with the way you would "normally" do things? What if the intuitive hit you received ran counter to what you thought was the right way? We privilege reason over all else, yet what if your rational thinking was actually getting in the way?

Enlightenment can be easy – if we are willing to put in the work. I believe that we get "lighter" by removing our burdensome beliefs and conditioning. Notice how you feel lighter when you're thinking clearly and energized, versus when you feel "stuck" in your thoughts. When we have limited beliefs taking up space in our mind, we can perpetuate that stuckness, because our mind literally can't see past the thought.

This catharsis of original conditioning is the "work" of enlightenment. In order to really "do the work," we must decide to move past that pre-existing programming that wasn't really ours to begin with and make the choice to move toward the intuitive part of ourselves that is online and waiting to be trusted. Essentially, it is a process of moving your mental model of validation and authority inward. When we let an external authority dictate our actions, we give away our ability to make an empowered decision for ourselves. If you are moving towards internal approval and acceptance, the first step is to say yes to what your intuition is communicating to you; however inconvenient.

Many of our rule-based systems operate on a fear of authority and punishment, so it's natural to feel some resistance when you start to reclaim space for yourself to speak. You might find that your new sovereignty doesn't sit so well with certain people, or that you now come off as abrasive. You might feel like you're operating "outside the rule book" or that you have no sense of control at first. All this is normal. Starting to let go of your normal conditioning will inevitably bring up all the fears of what will happen when your protections go away. Who will you be then? What will happen when you are the one in the driver's seat of your life?

Your Most Powerful Ally

This book is about building your relationship with your inner authority, which is your connection to Divine Authority. Your authentic, whole self *is* your divinity embodied. The more you cultivate this center, the more you will experience what you have always been seeking: liberation, independence, sovereignty, and joy. Why? Because your inner Divine Authority is your most powerful ally in life.

Isn't it interesting that the word divine has come to mean both the ability to prophesy and to be God-like? What is intuition if not the ability to know beyond the confines of the rational mind?

What if all the decisions you made from now on came from the most expansive perspective possible? What if you had a personal advocate who always wanted you to succeed by your side? What if you didn't have to waste time in conflict with yourself? What if you could accomplish, attain, and achieve those desires and dreams that not only serve your highest path but feel good? This might sound impossible to some of you, but it's not. It's very possible to live in alignment with your inner Divine Authority and come from your center. It's possible to live a life that feels graceful, easeful, and empowered even in the face of external chaos. It's possible to live in joy and be successful without burning yourself out.

The most important step now is to give yourself permission to live from this place. If you're here, it's because you are ready to begin or in the process of creating a relationship with your inner Divine Authority. You are ready to cultivate the tools and skills necessary to support you on this journey. You know that there will be some hard work ahead, and you are here for that.

Part of taking our power back is that we no longer wait for anyone else to give us permission. No one can tell you when you're ready. No one can do the work for you. When someone else tells you what to do, it disempowers your inner authority. Permission might seem passive, but it's important to communicate to yourself that you are ready to listen to your inner Divine Authority.

Once you have permitted yourself to live from this place, you must commit with your full being. I recommend declaring these statements out loud at the very least. State what you are committed to so you start embedding this vision into your reality. When you make a commitment to yourself, you are communicating your intention to the universe and your higher self; setting in motion a divine process that will serve your growth. Most importantly, you are claiming your role and responsibility in the process.

The next few chapters (Mind, Emotions, Body, Heart) will explore how we can bring both intellectual (left-brain) and intuitive (right-brain) intelligence to our process for a more embodied understanding and activation of our inner authority.

Because the material is so complex, I'm choosing to highlight a few key areas of research that are most relevant to the concepts and practices shared in this book. I am sharing the insights and ideas that have resonated for me in my journey and the techniques I've found to be supportive of my inner growth. I write what I practice and what I teach to others in my workshops and training. I will mention some people and theories that have inspired me to dig deeper into certain areas to better understand my assumptions and make more informed decisions. Every journey looks different. I've tried to share what I believe are invaluable and tested techniques, but you will only believe this yourself if you try them. Take what works and leave the rest, for ultimately, this book is teaching you how to cultivate *your* knowledge paths and develop trust in your intuition over time.

Reflection Questions:

1. What are some of my defining moments and why? What choice(s) was I presented with? What made this moment significant in the larger arc of my life story?

____

____

____

____

2. What am I giving myself permission to do or be moving forward?

____

____

____

____

3. What goals, intentions, or actions, am I committing to moving forward?

____

____

____

____

Actionable Practices:

1. List out the commitments you are making to yourself. Post this list somewhere you can see every day.

____

____

____

2. Create a beautiful ritual to honor your commitment ceremony. Find significant objects that make you feel powerful, create a vision board that catalyzes your desires, light a candle, and state your intentions. Anything you want! Get creative. Use this ritual to start playing with how you might speak to your inner Divine Authority.

____

____

____

3. Commit to a regular meditation practice for a week. If you are a beginner, try 5 minutes a day. If you are more advanced, challenge yourself to go deeper with your practice and technique.

____

____

____

Go Deeper:

1. *The Red Book* by Carl Jung

2. *The Artists' Way* by Julia Cameron

3. *Zen Mind, Beginner's Mind* by Shunryu Suzuki

CHAPTER 3

Wisdom of the Mind

Mantra:

I open to my whole brain intelligence.

I give myself permission to create from the place of no-mind.

I am both intelligent and intuitive.

I am connected to my transcendent intelligence.

I source knowledge from within.

Keywords:

Mind, Air, Breeze, Intelligence, Creative,
Invisible, Focus, Transcendent

You are hardwired for intuition. We are so deeply conditioned by our families, relationships, roles, and society at large to act and express in certain ways that many of us forget this fact. Some of us never knew it was an option. Many of us are taught that intuitive equals emotional, which is unwelcomed in most situations – especially professional ones. Thus, intuition is demoted, disregarded, and generally deemed untrustworthy. Few would say that intuition is a source of information and discernment, and thus are not able to access the full power of our innate, whole intelligence: intellectual *and* emotional, tactical *and* transcendent.

The mind is an invisible, dominating force in our lives. In Western culture, we emphasize knowledge that is rooted in fact, evidence, or empirical logic. We appreciate rational experiments and outcomes that can be replicated. Our mind is good at investigating, analyzing, strategizing, and solving problems. It's a lot more challenging to "prove" intuition, yet everyone has a sense of what this is for them.

I like to think that the mind is a precious *tool*. More importantly, it can be an invaluable ally if we know how to use its power constructively and objectively. After all, the mind is easily manipulated into believing things that feel good or confirming our existing, unconscious beliefs and biases. The mind lends itself well to conditioning, and anyone living inside of a culture is exposed to exactly that: ideas about what is "right" and what is "wrong" based on what they were taught. To some extent, we all operate within a framework of socio-cultural conditioning that contains and perpetuates a shared set of beliefs at multiple levels.

The relationship with the mind is thus a tricky one. This multifaceted tool is often abused and easily misunderstood, especially when you start to learn about the nature of your thoughts and their role in your experience of life. Thoughts form beliefs, many of which can be disempowering, especially when we aren't aware of them. The good news is that thoughts, beliefs, and biases can all be changed. Put another way, we can reprogram the invisible, mental fabric that creates our reality with the help of the *whole mind.*

Contemplate this: the word *mind* means "what we pay attention to." Thus, how we focus the mind determines much of what we "get." Do you like what you're getting out of life right now? Do you know *how* your mind is creating those results? If the mind is so important when it comes to executing on our vision, then why does it also limit us? How is it possible that our beliefs can both serve and stop us?

The mind is not an enemy. It is not something you have to battle or punish until it behaves better. It would be natural to assume that the mind has no place in the process when it comes to developing our intuition. Yet there is nothing further from the truth! It's time to reframe the role of the mind as we cultivate new levels of awareness.

The mind is not mutually exclusive of intuition and ultimately, we can't get to the heart of our intuition without the mind. By learning how to work with a whole-mind approach, you engage the left brain to access a new level of productivity, self-efficacy, and leadership while simultaneously accessing the discoveries, hidden genius, and innate creativity that live in your deeply powerful right-brain.

This begins with getting your rational mind "on-board." I learned that the best way to do this is by providing facts, evidence, research, and information that our brains can "digest" and understand. I'm not asking you to believe in something just because I say it. Both intellectual and intuitive discernment are the name of the game. Checking facts *and* checking in with yourself provide answers that make sense for *you*. This is what makes it so much fun to work with all of your faculties – it allows you to more easily integrate the parts of yourself that you might have originally believed were unwelcome in your life.

You're about to undertake a process I can best describe as the active rehabilitation of the fractured mind.

The Basics of the Brain

The most important distinction that I want to make right away is that your mind and your brain are not the same thing, although people tend to use these definitions interchangeably. So, let's start with a little science to set the context. The *brain* is a physical organ that processes information about our experience. The *mind* creates meaning about that experience based on our conditioned perceptions of the world. You can think of the brain as the hardware that transmits and receives data, and the mind as the operating system, or software, that runs your programs of reality. This immediately begs the question: where does intelligence originate and reside?

Brain Dominance Theory states that each hemisphere of the brain tends to specialize and preside over different functions, processes unique kinds of information, and deals with different kinds of problems. Your left brain is the home of language, numbers, and science. Your "logical" side of the brain uses reason and sequential thinking to evaluate and assess the world, loves analyzing, investigating and dissecting information, thinks in words, language, and numbers. It's ordered, organized, and highly functional; yet deeply rigid and controlled. The left brain likes to take information and place it within a linear frame of reference so that things "make sense." The left brain is active. This rational activity is the masculine polarity of the brain and the most prevalent mode of decision-making in the techno-analytical intellectualism of modern times.

The right side of the brain is intuitive, creative, and instinctive. It deals with emotions and thinks in pictures. Unlike the well-ordered rational left brain, the right brain doesn't follow a sequence; rather it embraces the non-dual relational nature of the whole. The domain of non-verbal music, art, imagination, and relationship, the right brain is spontaneous and free, spatial, and holistic in its understanding. Compared to the left brain, one might describe the right brain as passive. But that's only an illusion of dominant, left-brain thinking.

The right brain accesses and processes information based on experiences that have no causal relationship – in other words, it is a master at finding patterns and making connections between things that don't seem to be related. This is where innovations often occur, as the intuitive logic looks for resonance in new relationships. Right brain thinking is akin to sense-making: feeling into what wants to emerge organically. Conceptually, it is the whole that contains all opposites and unifies them in the greater field of connection. We see the right brain at work in holistic healing practices including creative non-verbal modalities such as movement or art therapy, in education, and in therapeutic traditions from around the world.

Both sides of the brain play critical and significant roles in how we learn, experience, and make sense of ourselves and our world. Our birthright is to operate consistently from a "whole-brain" state. This is the ability to simultaneously activate and access both sides of our cerebral cortex equally. Think of the "whole-brain" state as mental harmony, where you function seamlessly and effortlessly across the spectrum of thinking, learning, ideating, innovating, and creating. We use the whole-brain state daily. For example, both hemispheres work in conjunction for common tasks like having a conversation: the left is analyzing words and vocabulary while the right is processing context, tone, and nonverbal cues.

Yet a confluence of factors, including conditioning, often creates dominance in one hemisphere. Perhaps it was important to our parents that we became doctors, so we focused on left-brain activities that strengthened our linear thinking at the expense of our creative genius. Perhaps we grew up in a culture where order and rules were primary, so we focused on rational activities and jobs, roles, and careers. Throughout history and especially since the Industrial Age, creativity has been undervalued and suppressed in settings that emphasize a certain kind of intelligence over another. As individuals, we are not always conscious to the realization that we have prioritized a way of thinking and operating that is valued more than another simply because our family, friends, or culture said so. For many, in seeking validation, we often suppressed our creativity, imagination, and vision in order to belong, to be accepted, or to survive.

We also unconsciously prefer functions of the brain that get us what we want. Whether it's love from our partner or validation from a colleague, we tend to focus on the strategies that are proven – after all, if something big is on the line, we want to make sure we're investing in a solution that works. If certain habits or responses were validated for us growing up, we are more likely to use them in the future. You may have sought approval from a parent by getting good grades in school, so you find yourself studying your facts rigorously to get that raise or better position at work. Or, perhaps your family of origin valued hard work and your creative abilities were brushed off as a fanciful waste of time and so you stopped pursuing your love of drawing, painting, poetry or dance and took up accounting instead, appeasing expectations and ensuring you would be beyond reproach in your choice of vocation. We all employ different strategies to meet the internalized and often invisible needs buried deep in our psyches, yet we do this at the expense of other parts of ourselves, from innate gifts and talents to our dreams and visions.

Intellect vs Instinct: The Two Halves of the Human Brain

Admittedly, our Western culture tends to prioritize left brain thinking. If you were good in school and got a "real" job in a traditional career path like me, then you are most likely a left brain dominant person. However, in recent years, right-brain intelligence has made a roaring comeback. It is especially prevalent in disruptive industries such as technology, media, entertainment, and business innovation where new ideas and ways of doing things are deeply valued by stakeholders in the field. We use our right-brain thinking when the standard formula won't work, and we need to invent a new solution on the spot.

Design thinking is another trend that swept through the business world a few years back. While it follows an easy, replicable process, it's designed to cultivate innovation and new ideas. If you look at the explosion of technology, disruptive businesses, and entertainment over the last decade, you'll notice some obvious trends. Right-brain thinking is becoming far more valuable than it ever was, and rightly so, for these particular abilities connect us to our whole self.

Some believe that right-brain thinkers will rule the world. The truth is that no one specific mode of thinking is "better" than the other. Both are immensely valuable and the more they work together, the more we feel productive *and* connected to our full potential. Our world is asking us to cultivate our ability to respond in more innovative ways that are rooted in relational attunement with ourselves and others, as well as the earth. Because right-brain thinking is so much about sensing, synthesis, and distilling relationships, we often refer to it as divergent; for it's not about defining one path so much as opening up a possibility space that can take us to many new places.

Right-brain thinking is not how we *normally* think about thinking. Perhaps you conceptualize "thinking" as collecting and analyzing facts, arriving at an answer, deducing a strategy, or creating a solution for something. This answer is arrived at by a rigorous series of steps that are reductionist in nature: there is a clear and fixed definition of "right" in this situation. And there can only be one outcome.

Right-brain thinking, on the other hand, is far more syncretic; seeking to explore relationships and connections between things. Right-brained thinking is less fact and more insight. It sometimes arrives as a flash of inspiration to get that tune we've been singing on paper, or emerges in an evocative image we capture one day. Because we can't treat our inner muse like a math problem, the right side of the brain gets a bad rap for being dreamy and detached. Yet it serves as a valuable resource for the other analytical and active side of the brain.

The Space of Thought and No Thought

It turns out that we can't be constantly thinking – we need space to process our thoughts. This is called the Default Mode Network of the brain. The information we receive in the form of mental insights and intelligence needs to be processed and digested, usually while in some form of non-active thinking such as contemplation, reflection, or introspection. This is where we let the more "convergent" side of our brain (i.e. the left) turn off and the divergent one (i.e. the right) turn on. This is how we orient new information to our existing concepts and frameworks: through the process of allowing unconscious, transcendent intelligence to lead, which means our monkey mind needs to take a break. The average person has 6,200 thoughts a day. Space and time are necessary ingredients for imagination to emerge. Not giving ourselves the opportunity to sit with the information we receive cuts us off from accessing *all* available wisdom.

Many famous writers, inventors, poets, and thinkers like Einstein, Edison, Darwin, and J.K. Rowling were well known for their profuse daydreaming. Yet they weren't wasting time thinking about silly things as some might assume – or as some of us were admonished when we were young. Instead, they were naturally accessing their brain's Default Mode Network and speeding up their intuitive productivity. The "default mode" is the place where we solve problems, generate our best ideas, and make sense of our world and future. In essence: when you space out and let your mind wander, you're actually doing your best "thinking." Your mind can take you to some unexpected and intriguing places. Daydreaming is what futurist Rita King calls the "tedium of creativity" for it is when we are drifting through the mundane that inevitably we bump elbows with the miraculous.

Where does innovation come from though? Your brilliant ideas and breakthroughs are the result of a whole-brain approach that gives you both the active and "inactive" space to digest and sift through all the data coming in. It's not healthy to be in constant mental or creative overdrive because the best ideas bubble up in the silence of the mind when we least expect them. Isn't it funny how you recall the answer right when you stop trying to remember it? That's why.

In our modern world, we've made time into a commodity. This means your time is money, and when you're not making money you're not being "productive." So, we demonize time that isn't spent assuring or building our value as a contributing member of Western society. We pull ourselves up by our bootstraps and let talking heads convince us that working 100 hours a week for our dream makes sense. Yet time and time again, wiser traditions have nudged us to look deeper than that – and have provided simple methods to connect with that inner wisdom: meditation, mindfulness, and pranayama (breathing). We can meditate with an app now, and yet we still make excuses to avoid sitting with ourselves.

We've made it our life's work to be busy because that has become the definition of being.

If you want to know how to get the most out of your brain, then you need to give it space. Learning how to integrate both aspects of your brain's intelligence – the intellectual and the intuitive – will actually serve your productivity in the long run. When you give your brain the "passive" creative time to rest, sift, digest, daydream, and weave connections, you'll find that you generate more interesting and innovative breakthroughs. You'll find that it takes less force to be creative in general, because the information you've absorbed has been well composted into a fertile foundation for ideas to flourish. You might even reclaim aspects of your true nature that you didn't feel safe inhabiting so long ago.

You Are Creative

From a very young age, I became overidentified with my left-brain intelligence. With a more right-brain dominant sister holding the official title of "artist" in our family, I took on the role of "the smart one" who was expected to follow the "right path" – from getting "good grades" to having a "good career." Sound familiar? Or, perhaps you are the creative one – did you rebel against time management or basic business practices? Who did you decide you needed to be and what did you sacrifice in choosing sides? What "brain" did you identify with? Like muscles, certain functions atrophy if we don't use them. But this doesn't mean that they aren't there, that we can't recall them, or that we can't activate and integrate the wisdom of these parts to make ourselves whole. We are so much more powerful than when we operate at half capacity.

When I learned about the anatomy of the brain and gained a deeper understanding of how intelligence functions, it dawned on me that I possessed right-brain capabilities that had been underplayed over the course of my life. This is where my holistic personality, traits, and abilities flourished and took root. In fully acknowledging that I too was inherently creative, I stepped into power I didn't know I had. I gave myself permission to call myself a creative, to explore my creative impulses and questions, and to produce work that defied existing expectations. I explored corners of my psyche that I had kept off-limits from myself and how I expressed my potential in the world. This expanded my understanding of intelligence at a core level, and I was able to more deeply appreciate other forms of intellect and genius – both within myself and in others.

This knowledge taught me how to respect intelligence as a holistic set of attributes and abilities; a toolkit for making sense of the world that could be expanded and developed in multiple dimensions. My original understanding of intelligence as a purely left-brain function led me to see myself in a limited capacity, and my world reflected that. While I *was* still successful within that definition, I hadn't yet reached or unleashed the full potential of my authentic expression. Only when I stepped into a more holistic perspective of intelligence was I able to access more of my inner authority. I felt more comfortable and capable, more empowered to explore new possibilities, and experience new sides of myself. In other words, I flourished. It's amazing what happens when we accept ourselves and bring online the parts of us that were previously shunned.

We are wired in the brain to have access to our intuitive abilities. Most of us just haven't been taught how to use this ability, for it's been condemned to the realm of "woo" in our data-driven, left-brain dominant cultural conditioning. The occasional scientist is allowed to be eccentric because they can clearly validate their process through the sanctioned cultural conditions. Einstein, for example, was known for his eccentricity – and yet he is celebrated for his logic by history.

As you can see from a very simplified summary of the left and right brain, intelligence is broad and best approached through an integral perspective: one that considers how each part influences the whole. Whole-brain living gives us access to the infinite potential that resides inside: the visions, urges, impulses, wild ideas, and next-level innovations that percolate in our right-brain are given voice and expression through the action-oriented strategy of the left.

Where we are is always a powerful starting place. Take a moment and reflect on your own life. What side of the brain is more dominant for you? What abilities come more naturally for you? What were you praised for? What were you punished for? Are there any skills or strengths that you hide because they were deemed less important or unsavory? Is there anything that has been asking for your attention in your life? The more you explore and reflect on your current patterns and how they serve you, the easier it will be to see alternatives.

The Landscape of the Multi-Dimensional Mind

Now that we've talked about the brain, let's discuss the mind. The mind, as compared to the brain, is less tangible and generally still a matter of scientific debate. Nonetheless, it's vital to understand the workings of the mind.

In psychological theory, we have several minds functioning as one mind. The two primary minds are the conscious and the unconscious. The term subconscious is also used interchangeably with unconscious. I'm going to use the term "unconscious mind" but if the term subconscious resonates, then I encourage you to go with what works for you. These two aspects of our mind are interdependent and interconnected and play a role in how we perceive the world. Let's break it down.

The conscious mind is volitional: it takes action on our will. The conscious mind sets goals and objectives, judges outcomes, and makes decisions. It can think abstractly and process complexity. It is the master of rationalization. This is the part most of us think of when we think of our mind. Would it blow your mind to know that your conscious "online mind" is only about 5% of your total consciousness?

The unconscious mind is where we store at least 95% of our waking life, for it's basically a recording device that remembers your most necessary life functions. Every time your heart beats you don't need to think about *how* to do that - you just do it because your unconscious already knows.

How does the "offline mind" know how to run the body's functions, and remember how to move? The unconscious is insanely powerful – about 10,000 times more powerful than the conscious mind. But it requires programming, which is why the unconscious gets a bad rap: all your early conditioning is stored here. Habitual processes like how to chew your food but also your origin stories, your beliefs, your sense of self, your outlook on the world, your views about other people and how you relate, and your experience of emotions as they were experienced by a much younger, developing self.

Most of our learned behaviors, attitudes, patterns, and deep beliefs are programmed by the age of 7 and internalized as "reality." These beliefs become the filters through which we view all things.

The more emotionally charged a situation, the more likely it will be stored in the mind for future reference – both positive and negative, depending on the emotional charge around them. After all, the human body is wired to survive, and that means eliminating perceived threats. So, if we received our core conditioning in an environment that caused us pain, we are more likely to imprint trauma and remember it in our bodies, even if we can't remember or recall it with our minds. This is so that later we will automatically (i.e. unconsciously) choose to protect ourselves. This is one of the ways that our unconscious mind starts to create limitations in our life. This illustrates how our past unconsciously influences our present, all without our *volition*. This unconscious patterning, called "repetition compulsion," leads us to repeat circumstances that confirm our worldview – thus enacting them over and over. Or, we can choose to consciously intercept the pattern in the present and design different outcomes for ourselves, thus overcoming painful childhood imprints.

All of the deep conditioning we are trying to address exists in the unconscious – the most challenging place to navigate. As you can see, it's a vast, limitless and mysterious place that contains so much of our potential and true power. We don't usually think about the unconscious until we're prompted – after all, why would we? We don't feel its presence in the same way we hear our chatty mind speak. Yet the unconscious has almost complete control over our (perception of) life and the results we get. It issues silent directives that "make" us create the opposite of what we think we want (i.e. our conscious mind). This leaves us believing all the familiar limiting thoughts: that we aren't imaginative, creative, smart, beautiful, successful, or worthy.

Let me pause to say one thing before we go further: I'm drawing attention to that which hinders because we're all trying to get past our limitations. But keep in mind that what's in our unconscious is not all bad! There is a ton of good in there, including beliefs, behaviors, and habits that make you YOU in all the best ways. Let's take a moment to honor that, and honor ourselves. We're always seeking to improve and to evolve; it's our natural inclination to do so. But we sometimes forget to notice and acknowledge the goodness; the successes and the positive attributes about ourselves.

This chapter is designed to illuminate how the mind creates conditions, and how you can consciously condition the mind to better support your own growth. This starts in the unconscious. Our beliefs create and enforce our conditioning, so working to clarify what they are now will help you see yourself: your current limitations as well as your strengths. Your conditioning is only your *unconscious* thought patterns, which can be reprogrammed by making them conscious and working with them. When we don't examine an internalized belief – such as a story that "I can't be an engineer because I didn't go to the right university" for example – we allow it to go unchecked in our behaviors, and to ultimately control our lives. Conditioning is hard to see at first, which makes it easy to run on autopilot in the background. It's also self-reinforcing: we believe what we see, and we are seeing what we believe.

Where Our Beliefs Come From

Beliefs are the meaning we make around our experiences. Beliefs define our view of ourselves and the world. Over time, with enough reinforcement, these beliefs become fixed behaviors. Changing beliefs can change how we experience life. For example, if you hold the belief that you are unlucky, you will most likely have experiences that confirm that belief; you will filter and perceive your "unlucky" experiences in this way. This invites an investigation: Did the belief reinforce itself? Did the thought "I am unlucky" make it happen? Are your thoughts unlucky? Are your thoughts true?

You probably don't notice the simple fact that you are bombarded by thousands of thoughts a day. Most of them aren't that important and let's face it: most of them are unconscious. When you think to yourself "shut the door" on our way out of the house, you don't herald that as a breakthrough because you don't notice it as a unique or memorable thought.

A thought, objectively, is just a thought. It's like a cloud passing across the sky. However, it is the attached beliefs and reactions to a thought (either conscious or unconscious) that creates an experience of immense joy or immense suffering. Which means that a belief has more power than one of your average daily thoughts. A belief is a whole story of interrelated thoughts, experiences, memories, impressions, and emotions that operate invisibly, yet inevitably set the foundation for who we are. The more we act upon our existing beliefs, the more we reinforce neurological pathways in our brains that perpetuate those beliefs, our behavioral patterns, and the manifestations they create in our lives.

Notice when you tell yourself "I am not _________." Is that a belief or a thought? Why do you believe that?

And when did you first start to believe that thought? Was that original thought a result of a situation that's no longer true for you now? If so, it might be time to update your beliefs, so they reflect your current thoughts and reality. This is a powerful process to take yourself through when you find yourself creating a limitation. Ask yourself: Where did that thought come from? Do I truly believe it? How old is it? Who was involved? How did this belief serve me before? How does it serve me now? If it's not serving me, what's stopping me from changing my belief or updating my behaviors?

One of the most prevalent beliefs I encounter is: I am not intuitive. This is often part of conditioning children receive as they are socialized. Have you ever been told you were weird because you had intuitive insights? Did you ever share something that scared someone because they didn't understand how you knew this? Were you shamed for having an imaginary friend or just for talking to yourself? This happens all too often, especially when we are young, and when it does, we reject and hide our intuitive abilities.

When I was a child, I had a well-developed intuitive sense. I knew how certain situations would play out and I could foretell a likely outcome. I felt everything, often picking up on others' emotions. I instinctively understood people's intentions; I could "see" right through them. I was making predictions and engaging in conversations that made adults uncomfortable, which got me punished, shamed, and shunned. So, I shut it down. I put on the "cloak of normality" so I wouldn't be rejected or ridiculed anymore.

Many of us are taught that our intuitive knowledge and curiosity must abide by a set of rules that are enforced through some form of punishment if we color outside the lines. If we don't believe in our intuition, we will inevitably experience some disconnection from it in real life. We will find it hard to trust ourselves fully and listen when we hear a message from our inner authority. Noticing what stories you are telling yourself about what is possible is the first step to cultivating a better sense of intuition with yourself. What are your beliefs about yourself and your intuitive abilities? Do you notice any stories emerging?

It wasn't until I began to release some of my big, life-shaping beliefs that this formative memory arose. I had no idea I had made such a choice to become "normal," but as the information flooded my conscious awareness, I understood why I did: to avoid pain and to protect myself. We protect ourselves to survive and conform in an attempt to thrive. But without our full capabilities, without our intuition, we are not embodying the full spectrum of our "intelligence" or accessing all our abilities. Intuition is the ability to understand *faster* than the speed of thought. In fact, intuition requires no thinking at all.

An obsessive mind that takes no action is unproductive, for it doesn't put the mind in service to action. Overthinking is a productivity killer and confusion generator. Projecting into the future can be fun, but it can also be equally unproductive, especially if it prevents us from being present with our life now.

Powerful Tools for the Mind

When we clear unnecessary thinking and limiting beliefs, we open up space for more inner authority to emerge and show us the way forward. The unconscious mind is where we integrate and uncover our deep-set patterns. However, it isn't always so easy to consciously "choose" a different thought or change a belief because the unconscious computer is running its usual program and it doesn't easily take direction from the conscious mind. After all – it's easier to go on autopilot.

Thoughts are anchored in place by emotion, trauma, and environmental imprinting. This is a key reason why affirmations are often ineffective and/or require a lot of time to create desired change. Every time we even do something as simple as recognize that we're in an old belief or pattern, we're interrupting the conditioning and actively changing the neural network of the brain and allowing new networks to be formed. In neuroscience, they say that neurons that fire together, wire together, and that is why beliefs become so entrenched. The same is true when we're consciously forming new neural pathways. When we choose to think alternatively and choose different actions, we begin to establish new neurological pathways and lessen the strength of the old ones. This is a process that does not occur overnight.

Most people give up when they don't experience change quickly enough. In my experience of giving up many times, I didn't have the right tools and support – and I was unwilling to ask for help from people who have dedicated their lives to this type of work. One of the best ways to gain access to your unconscious is through assisted work with a trained practitioner. Psychology and therapy are well-known modalities that can support working with the unconscious mind to interrupt habitual mentalities, clear limiting beliefs, and empower constructive and life-affirming thoughts, behaviors, and experiences.

There are many modalities that work with the body to reach the unconscious mind and reprogram or release the mental material that no longer serves us. Psych-K is a modality that uses a simple whole-brain approach to quickly harmonize the left and right hemispheres of the brain. This allows the conscious mind to communicate with and reprogram the unconscious mind. I've been able to work through negative narratives, limiting beliefs, false memories, old emotions, and other unconscious material that was causing me to suffer and holding me back.

It was so remarkable in its ease, speed, and effectiveness that I became certified as a Psych-K facilitator. This framework also engages another aspect of the mind to effectuate our conscious, desired changes – the Superconscious Mind. This is the ultimate knower, observer, seer, and facilitator of our life's unfolding. The superconscious correlates to the Atman, Higher Self, Great Spirit, Soul, or Inner Divine Authority. Engaging the whole mind and creating a harmonious, open channel between hemispheres of the brain successfully reprogram outdated beliefs. An added benefit is that the whole-brain engagement helps to develop a stronger connection to intuition and clear transmission of a transcendent intelligence.

Meditation is an essential practice for developing your ability to access all levels of the mind. There are many documented benefits to meditation, notably the harmonization of brain waves that allow us to calm a frazzled mind, get focused, learn quicker, or access other states of consciousness. During deep meditation, the brain will produce theta waves, as our senses are withdrawn from the outside world and we are focused on signals originating within. Theta state is a "gateway" to intuition; it is a liminal, "in-between" state where we can access visions, intuition, and information beyond our conscious awareness.

Consistent meditation more easily allows you to intentionally enter powerfully productive brainwave states where new neurological pathways are activated. As you find stillness in the body and steadiness in the breath, the chatter of the mind fades. Pay no attention to what passes; let it rise and fall away, and you begin to notice the essence behind the thoughts and the identity. You enter the transitional and transformative space; the threshold between your waking self and super-consciousness.

If all of this information about the brain, the mind(s), thoughts, thinking, conditioning, and beliefs is confusing, I'd like to share an important truth that helped me cut to the heart of the matter when my head was about to explode. The most important and underused function of the conscious mind is intentional awareness: bringing our focused attention to how we are using our mind's power. The power of focus, when correctly harnessed, is a superpower. Focus transcends all thinking, harmonizes all functions, and integrates every aspect of our being in service to the task, problem, or matter at hand. A busy mind is *not* a productive mind. A focused mind is unstoppable.

Engaging the Mind as an Ally

When we decide we want to better understand our internal conditioning and shift our behaviors, we have to harness both parts of our mind: the conscious and the unconscious. In the conscious mind, we first identify conditioning, examine whether it still serves your current reality, and decide whether to keep it or release it. This is an active process that incorporates dedicated self-awareness, self-observation, self-inquiry, and reflection over time. It can also help us to communicate with the people in our life about our perceived challenges in order to better see our blind spots.

It's good to challenge and question the information that filters into your world – that's part of developing your inner authority. For a long time, I struggled to accept many spiritual teachings that contradicted what I had believed to be true my entire life. I didn't know how to assess who was more "right" in situations or what I believed in response. This led me to investigate, research, and contemplate my biases and assumptions. It didn't lead me directly to answers and that helped me make critical distinctions about what resonated as true for me. We shouldn't believe something just because it sounds good or confirms a bias. Discernment is an important function of the rational mind. Consider what the new information challenges, or what beliefs it contradicts. What stories does it trigger within you? What leads you to automatically accept or dismiss this information?

When you start to question why a certain piece of information resonates with you in a certain way, inevitably you will begin to uncover your foundational story or set of beliefs: the biases and assumptions that fuel your actions, habits, and behaviors. Naming the original ideas and biases is an important part of challenging your foundational conditioning. Throughout this process, imagination is just as important as reason, for we cannot build a new reality for ourselves if we cannot envision what that next level looks and feels like. Our reason cannot create this alone. Rather, it serves the vision and carries it forward.

The reality is that we can't evolve without our mind. As I've mentioned, it's helpful to think of the mind as a tool. Just like any tool, we need to practice and refine our skills using it. This is part of the process of personal mastery. When we stop being slaves to our pre-programmed mind – in other words, following it blindly – we find our freedom. The mind can imprison us with rules, beliefs, old stories, painful judgments...or it can unleash untold imagination, artistry, and innovation. With commitment, discipline, and trust, you harmonize the mind and direct it in service to your dreams, desires, and visions.

Productivity is simply the manifestation of your potential in service to your highest vision. When we limit our potential, we cramp our productivity. We diminish our inner authority, and this serves no one – least of all yourself. It's not your fault that you were raised a certain way or had certain privileges or none at all. It's not your fault that your parents had their own conditioning to deal with and most likely this impacted you on some level. It's just the way that conditioning works. As a consequence, we disconnect from critical internal resources like our intuition, our sovereignty, our creativity, and our sense of self-worth because we feel powerless to our conditioning.

One of the most empowered perspectives possible is that you are not a victim of your life circumstances. What if it's not a mistake that you grew up a certain way, learned what you learn, or acquired the beliefs, biases, and perspectives that you hold? Viewed from a higher level, you might begin to see that these conditions were specifically created (some might say "chosen") for your growth. Learning how to break free from our limiting beliefs is what ultimately allows us to choose another form more in alignment with the power that is unique to each of us and this can only be discovered when we go beyond thoughts and concepts of who we think we should be. This is how we evolve into the best versions of ourselves.

For anyone who has suffered greatly, this might be a painful thing to hear. In no way do I intend to diminish anyone's very real lived experience, which I cannot claim to know. I can only speak to what I have seen when I have risen above my own pain to witness how the situation has been in service to my growth.

It's easy to feel victimized, especially if we feel misunderstood. Internalizing other people's opinions, expectations, and judgments is like ingesting poison. I know this all too well. After an unexpected and painful experience around online trolling, I had to dig deeper than ever to find the courage and conviction that I had at other times in my life.

A well-known motivational media company used the footage from the public talk I gave about leaving my first marriage to make a short-form video of my story. It spoke to the human condition through my personal story: the way I sacrificed my inner voice to appease others, seeking love and validation at the expense of my heart's knowing. When the video was released, it quickly went viral. Within a week it had 4 million views; after 3 months, 35 million views and over 250,000 shares. This unexpected success came with a dark downside – vicious comments. I wasn't prepared for them.

When I committed to giving my talk I decided to share a very personal story. I shared the defining moment: the lightning that struck me with such force I was suddenly jolted awake to the truth of my existence. I shared the lessons I learned about the importance of honoring myself and breaking free from a life that on the surface appeared perfect; yet underneath was fraught with suffering. I wasn't prepared for the response: an outpouring of pain, heartbreak, wounding, and the projection of hatred and shame onto me. The first DM I received said it all: "You're a fake, you're a fraud. Shame on you!" Over 90,000 comments sparked intense discussions about love, relationships, obligation, promises, independence, self-love, self-respect, selfishness, and the pain that in one way or another, we've all felt in our search for love and validation of our worth.

Amidst the spiteful comments, messages, and even death threats from complete strangers, I also received hundreds of heartfelt messages from many people, mostly women, who thanked me for the courage I had to say what no one had ever said before. They shared their stories. So many told me they thought they were the "only ones," and who were living with self-imposed shame, a broken heart, and a heavy spirit. I had broken the seal of shame by sharing my experience.

The truth is: while my story angered many, it healed a multitude more. Though at first, the shock and heartbreak I experienced from the trolling hurt me deeply, eventually I came to understand one of the most powerful truths of life: what we go through is not just for our healing – it's for those who hear our story and see themselves within it. The wisdom we extract from our most challenging, defining moments is meant to be shared. I lived that experience in my bones, but the story is not "mine." When we break through our pain, we pave the way for others to do the same.

The most remarkable realization I had through this experience was that by standing my ground, speaking my truth, and taking responsibility for my own decision, I inadvertently made myself a villain in the eyes of strangers who needed a "good enough reason" for me to leave my marriage. When they didn't hear it – when they didn't hear that I was a victim – they immediately lashed out at me. But I wasn't the victim. I didn't blame my ex-husband for anything, because there was no one to blame. I was also not in need of rescuing. I took an unconventional path, both in my decision to leave the relationship and in my decision to tell it. I shared my inner process of self-observation to dismantle the limiting beliefs, toxic expectations, and cultural conditioning that led to many decisions I had made with the right intentions, for the wrong reasons. When we don't want to hurt or disappoint others, we often hurt ourselves. I know I did.

No one deserves the "bad stuff" that happens to them. But we do get to choose how we orient to the challenges that are presented to us throughout life. The conditioning we are born into is fertile ground for our growth, for it shows us what wants to be healed if we are willing to learn the terrain. Until we are conscious of the way our mind is wired and what lives within, we will struggle to understand our external world and what it reflects to us. Your most powerful tool then is your perspective.

Compassion Begins in the Mind

When we first start to work with the mind, it can be easy to respond with self-judgment. You will notice more things that present as problems or things that "are wrong with you." You'll notice emotions and ideas that you swallowed long ago. You might feel like there's a lot to fix in your world or that you've waited too long to take action so that now there's a lot to clean up and it's overwhelming.

Judgment and self-criticism cut you off from intuition. You condemn yourself for what you didn't know at the time. When you are overly critical, you shut down your capacity to engage in the kind of non-linear, creative thinking that empowers your ability to generate innovative solutions and ideas. If you're too busy overthinking the outcome and blaming yourself for not seeing this sooner, you are probably too busy noticing the problems instead of seeing the opportunities being presented.

When I began to understand that I was having a deep awakening but didn't know what tools, knowledge, or resources to use to support myself, I turned to spiritual teachers and classic texts to find answers. And they all pointed to the logical, linear thoughts and my mind as the source of all my problems and suffering. Since I always valued my mind, my thinking abilities, and my intellect, this led to a lot of *unproductive* judgment towards myself. I shamed myself for being part of the problem (actually, the source of it) by perpetuating fantasies of success that were built on false ideas of how the world actually worked. I felt bad for enjoying my success and finding personal satisfaction in my life, even though many teachings pointed to the fact that it was some form of attachment. I had believed in a good life that was, according to some, an illusion. I was utterly confused.

Yet this experience of self-doubt and judgment opened me to a place of deep healing. It supported me in clarifying and updating my values, developing more compassion for myself and others, and bringing more heart-centered action into my work. It took three years to finally see that I wasn't a bad person for my decisions – like choosing a financial career, then leaving it to become an entrepreneur. I'm not an evil, heartless capitalist because I value financial stability, am savvy with money, and I desire to help others to make more empowered investment decisions.

You don't know everything you don't know until you wake up, and then suddenly it feels like someone turned on the floodlights in your dirty basement. It's called waking up or "becoming conscious" because that's what happens. We use our newfound awareness to make different, more empowered, and fundamentally life-affirming choices that support us in cultivating more aligned lives. Don't waste your time judging yourself. You are taking precious energy away from your own self-development.

When you uncover your internalized conditioning and limiting beliefs, you will gain a bigger picture of yourself. You will become more powerful simply because you have more data to work with. It can be humbling to realize that you've been defining your actions based on an outdated or incomplete idea of yourself. It's normal to have invisible biases operating below the surface (after all, there are 188 of them!) but you are responsible for how you choose to work with the information available to you at all times.

I've found that the more I learn, investigate, and explore, the more it requires an open mind. It's good to be a skeptic who's willing to be wrong about what they thought was right. This will strengthen your mind as it cultivates your willingness to grow past your edge. As you have hopefully noted, the mind can support you in making sense of the instincts, impulses, and urges that bubble up from your unconscious and taking mindful action on what matters.

My invitation to you is to consider how you filter information and apply experience. Do you consider what rings true or resonates with you, even if you don't understand it at first? Inevitably, our knowledge gaps push us to evolve outside of our comfort zone. We have to get bigger to fill in the holes. Not all the information we encounter will work for us, but it's important that you take a moment and ask yourself how you can learn from it. We aren't competing for accolades or awards. We earn our advancement by becoming aligned at our deepest levels of embodiment.

Reflection Questions:

1. How are you using your conscious mind? What are you thinking about? Are you ruminating? Are you projecting into the future? Are you creating anxiety or fear? What stories, thoughts, and worries are currently present?

____

____

____

____

2. What is your relationship with knowledge, learning, and not-knowing? How much emphasis do you place on outside expertise versus your own lived experience?

____

____

____

____

3. What's your relationship to intellect and intelligence? What is your experience of thinking? What happens when you're trying to figure something out and can't?

____

____

____

____

Actionable Practices:

1. The best way to discover limiting beliefs is to write down what you think about yourself. This will quickly expose your current self-limiting beliefs. Use the following exercise for identifying beliefs, thoughts, and assumptions:

   a. WHEN I DO ______ THEN ______.

   b. WHEN I ______ THEN I AM ______.

   c. WHEN I ______ I WILL GET ______.

   d. WHEN SOMEONE LIKE THIS ______ DOES THIS______, THEN IT MEANS ______.

   e. Now ask yourself: Are these statements true? Have they always been true? How do you know for sure?

   ____

   ____

   ____

   ____

   f. Now ask yourself, "What would I rather believe?" List these new beliefs.

   ____

   ____

   ____

   ____

2. Change the Belief

    a. From the exercise above, pick one belief/statement you want to change. Write down a list of 3 simple actions you can take to integrate this new empowering belief more firmly in your world.

    ____

    ____

    ____

    ____

    b. Take action! Consistent action changes the neurological pathways in our brains. This helps us deconstruct and repattern beliefs, modalities, and habits.

    ____

    ____

    ____

    ____

3. Select one of your defining moments from the Chapter 2 exercises. With your journal or note-taking device at the ready, write down what spontaneously comes up when you ask yourself:

    a. What did I believe before the defining moment?

    ____

    ____

    ____

b. Did that belief change? If so, how? If not, how can it change now?

____

____

____

____

c. Write out a detailed description of the belief – then and now. Review what's changed, and what has been transformed. With every instance of transformation or release of an old belief, say, "I honor your role in helping me understand my true power."

____

____

____

____

Go Deeper:

1. *Biology of Belief* by Bruce Lipton

2. *A Whole New Mind* by Daniel Pink

3. Psych-K: *www.psych-k.com*

CHAPTER 4

Wisdom
of the Emotions

Mantra:

I give myself permission to feel all my emotions and feelings.

I give myself permission to feel uncomfortable.

I give myself permission to express my emotions.

I allow myself to be free from doing.

I allow myself to be.

Keywords:

Emotions, Feelings, Water, Dissolution,

Depth, Oceanic, Expansion, Acceptance, Flow

We are taught to think that mind and emotion are totally incongruent. One is the realm of intelligence and the other is the realm of intangibility. One is welcomed, encouraged, and applauded. The other is the unwelcomed, suppressed, and avoided. However, both are necessary in providing a complete picture that helps us make more informed, conscious decisions about how we show up for ourselves and for the world.

Emotions are an important source of intuitive insight that can be consciously used to create better outcomes for yourself and your life. This is the true essence of productivity. When we acknowledge and accept our emotions and their inherent nature, we give ourselves the opportunity to experience the potential information they contain, rather than give in to the fear or discomfort they might otherwise provoke.

In the last chapter on the Mind, I described how humans are wired to be intuitive. Both our brain and our body is designed to support multiple forms of intelligence and data gathering in order to make sense of our complex world, but it is up to us to find our agency and use all that is available to us. What we perceive as "thinking" is simply one form of data; our emotions are another.

Just like the mind, our emotions allow us to gain insight into our rich and complex inner landscape. We feel our emotions arise as impulses, desires, and urges that reflect our personal experience back to us. These impulses are transmitted through the intelligent systems of the human body as signals. Just like a thought, emotions are another "invisible" way our transcendent intelligence centers communicate key pieces of vital data to us.

Emotions are powerful – often overpowering, sometimes uncomfortable, and mostly inconvenient to a linear, industrial, mechanistic definition of productivity. Because of this, emotions are easily dismissed as "irrational" or prioritized after facts. In fact, they are mostly deprioritized altogether.

Yet emotions are not so easily categorized, and that is why they provoke such complex and occasionally challenging experiences within us. Emotions present a key problem to the hierarchical, authoritarian system of mind: emotions can make us feel out of control, but that is only an illusion of the ego that prefers the safety of conformity over the full expression of inner authority. We're not trying to *control* emotions with the mind, we're learning to *notice* and *observe* emotions with our conscious awareness.

Emotions are a way in which you intimately connect to yourself as a human being. They also serve as cathartic releases for our system, for they cleanse our consciousness from trapped feelings and thoughts, old patterns, and stories. They show us where we are most alive or holding back; where we have experienced a violation or a rupture of trust. When we feel our emotions fully, we touch into depths that defy the mind.

Contrary to popular conditioning, listening to your emotions isn't silly or weak. Rather, it relieves your system of internalized pressure that builds up over time, resulting in blockages and dis-ease in the body. The more you allow your emotions to flow through you and listen, the more you will learn about what you want and how to take action. As you align more deeply with who you are, you will naturally embody more joy, acceptance, equanimity, and love within yourself.

Using the principle of awareness that we established in the last chapter, we're going to now apply it to the emotional realm. In this chapter, we'll explore how your permission to allow and embrace the fullness of your existence will support you in creating the success you desire. Many people have a distorted relationship with their emotions, leading to the suppression of authentic agency that inhibits your ability to step into your inner authority. When this happens, we are operating at half-capacity. When we suppress emotions, it creates internal imbalances that extend into our real life and impact others around us. And if we don't allow ourselves to feel our emotions, we certainly can't hear our intuition.

Take a minute now and reflect on your current relationship with your emotions. Do you feel that you are too emotional? Have you been told this? Or do you lean on the logical left-side of your brain to figure things out for you? If you have a complicated relationship with your emotions, you are not alone. Many people believe that they shouldn't show emotion or share their feelings. Much of this depends on which feelings, if any, were acceptable in our family of origin. And whether you are a man or a woman, our dysfunctional social norms view emotions as a liability: women are told not to express their emotions, and men are told not to feel them.

We can't see our emotions, making it easy to suppress and stuff them down. How does one quantify an emotion? We can't measure the impact of our emotional experience with tangible, concrete evidence the same way we establish facts. Yet if you learn to see the symptoms, you will inevitably start to notice the "invisible" impact of emotions in your life. Distorted and suppressed emotions show up in a myriad of ways: physical and psychological health issues, unfulfilling relationships, lack of productivity or inability to manifest our desires, a sense of being lost or purposeless, a constant longing for "something" – a type of unrest that is distracting at best and destructive at its worst. Make a commitment now, throughout this chapter, to work compassionately with your emotions. Consciously choose to address your emotional reactive patterns to enlighten and to release attachment for the actualization of your highest potential.

If you find that you have a limited vocabulary (which is almost anyone who isn't a therapist), there is a helpful tool called a Feelings Wheel, which you can easily find online. Expanding the range of words helps to refine feelings and better describe our experience. As you engage with more descriptive terms, notice any changes in your self-inquiry process. You may even choose to keep a feelings journal, or use a mood tracker, to help yourself "see" your feelings better.

The process by which you work with your emotions is simple: They want to be observed (1), acknowledged (2), accepted (3), fully felt and experienced (4), released (5), and finally, integrated (6) by reflecting on the lessons and gifts that these experiences impacted on our lives. Before we dive deeper into this process, let's start by exploring how our biology informs our emotional experience.

Emotions Are Natural

Emotions have a home and a role in our biology. We can't observe and measure our emotions the same way we would with physical phenomena, and this has made it challenging to consider emotions as a form of intelligence in the scientific world. However, a lot has changed over the years, and new developments in neuroscience demonstrate that emotion is biologically built into the body. In fact, we have a bonafide "emotional brain," which is as intricate as it is intelligent.

The emotional brain isn't one organ. It's an interconnected structure called the limbic system, which evolved about 150 million years before the cortex did – i.e. our "thinking" brain that we rely so much on. The limbic system governs primal instinct, feeling, and emotion. The main components of the limbic system are the hypothalamus (which controls the homeostatic mechanisms of the body), the pituitary gland (which regulates the hormones of the body), and the amygdala (which monitors sensory data for emotional content). The amygdala is responsible for the perception of emotions such as anger, fear, and sadness. It also controls our aggression. The amygdala is like a database. It stores memories of events and emotions so that you can recognize similar events in the future and adapt. Because the amygdala recognizes patterns and is designed to help regulate our flight or fight response, it plays a key role in the evaluation and recognition of potential threats.

The neuroscience of emotions was broadly expanded through the work of Dr. Candace Pert, an internationally recognized neuroscientist and pharmacologist who was a significant contributor to the emergence of "mind-body" medicine as an area of legitimate scientific research in the 1980s. Dr. Pert's work revealed that the limbic system is located throughout the body, not just in specific regions of the brain. The body has other powerful centers that receive and process emotional information. These "hot spots" are anatomically located in places where there is a lot of neurological activity – like the gut and the heart, both of which have their own neural network, a.k.a. brain cells! What this communicates is that emotions are processed through a vast network of receptors in the body – they don't originate in one place. These nodal points are designed to receive and interpret subtle signals and information, and our bodies express this information in right-brain capacities and physical sensation. Put another way, our *entire* body is emotional and processes emotional signals constantly.

Advances in neuroscience have provided us with a richer understanding of emotions and how they are here to work *with* us, not against us. Having emotions is human, plain and simple – so it's important that we honor them, observe them, learn from them, and integrate them so we can effectively benefit from their inherent wisdom. Shutting down, suppressing your emotions, hiding them, acting like they aren't important, or generally pretending like they don't exist is a mistake that we've all made too many times. Emotions are data; acting like they don't matter in our decision-making ignores the doorway they present to us in order to peer deeply into our inner world.

It was in 2016 that I had a mirror event to the defining moment that had given me the full-body, emotional breakdown that led me to leave my first marriage. After pouring my heart and soul into the start-up I had joined as "Employee #1" as the Chief Marketing Officer – helping to grow it from 4 people to an industry leader

– a change in the company's direction put me at odds with the new CEO. He and I were like oil and water. Our confrontations tore away at my self-confidence and the visionary abilities that had helped me establish the company (and myself) in the growing fintech industry. I loved what we had accomplished and the culture I had defined and nurtured. That made it easier to give up all my free, personal time, including my daily yoga practice, to go all-in with 100+ hour weeks and constant travel. My life felt like I was riding a bicycle downhill with no brakes. My Sunday yoga practice was my only solace; a sacred space to touch base with myself. On a Sunday in September, as I left the studio feeling at peace, I found a voicemail from the CEO on my phone. As I sat in the car and listened to it, I began to weep. I don't remember the content of the message and I don't remember how long I sat there and cried. All I remember is that I knew, "I couldn't do this any longer." It was the same impulse, the same message, the same knowing that had spoken so strongly to me once before. Once again, it was impossible to ignore.

The next day I had a conversation with the CEO, and we began the amicable process of my transition out of the company. I found that I had limitless opportunities to begin anew, many of which I had never before considered because I was too invested in fighting to make things work a certain way. I had ignored a multitude of signals, especially emotional ones, that were urging me to listen, to notice my emotional state, my lack of inspiration, and the misplaced but honorable sense of loyalty I had to that company and the people in it, whom I loved dearly.

Instincts & Emotional Behavior

Instincts are powerful mechanisms that operate beneath our conscious awareness and play an important role in our survival and other physiological responses. Honing our instinctive nature can unlock fear patterns we didn't know we had and unleash our self-awareness. Do you trust your primal instincts?

Instincts are a natural physical and emotional response that occur much faster than rational thinking. There is a half-second delay between an instinct and an associated thought that registers in our conscious awareness. If we were to think about a danger first, then react, we'd be dead. The mechanism of intuitive instinct ensures our survival by attaching a strong emotion to an experience that feels like "'danger." This mechanism hasn't gone away just because we no longer live as hunter-gatherers fending off predators. It exists in perpetuity as part of our human biology. However, our lives today present different danger signals that keep our survival instincts on high alert all the time, even though we're not in actual, imminent danger.

Stress triggers that danger signal, and most of us are under some form of constant stress from our daily lives. It ranges from environmental pollutants, toxins, and processed foods, to lifestyle factors, dietary and physical stress, to the most notable: the pressures of modern life, which include balancing work with personal life, relationships, deadlines, commuting, managing career and family, financial worries, or dealing with ongoing discrimination or bullying. These send our systems on alert and put us on edge. Globally, our stress levels went to red alert with the onset of the COVID-19 pandemic in 2020 – as did our emotions.

During that challenging season, in a blink of an eye, life was turned upside down and suddenly a lot of feelings came bubbling to the surface. Many of us faced our most challenging emotions in palpable ways that couldn't be denied. Think about your emotional reactions when COVID-19 became real for you. How did you react? How did you feel? How did that influence your thinking, your beliefs, your outlook? It's safe to say everyone's emotions were in overdrive. Disbelief, fear, anger, and reactivity got the best of us, and almost everyone I knew was triggered into unfamiliar and very powerful survival mechanisms and strategies. What did you learn about your emotional responses and your instincts?

I observed my emotional and mental state go from curiosity to concern, and finally into worst-case-scenario. In the face of so much uncertainty, my rational mind had no precedent and no anchor. I felt fear, worry, and anxiety no matter how much I meditated, and no amount of research or analysis helped me feel a sense of control. Though I can laugh about it now, I prepared for an end-of-the-world scenario; stocking up on canned and frozen foods, protein powders, and even water purification tablets. I was rationing our food intake to the point that I started monitoring Andrew's trips to the fridge! My survival instincts had taken over and put me on an uncomfortable edge. I was acting ridiculously at times, but my aggressive approach also helped me to feel like I was doing *something*. Taking action felt good.

It took a lot of self-observation and awareness to work through the emotional material that came up and to sift through irrational fears to find the seeds of truth about my deeper, transcendent nature. How could I find peace, what gave me real security, what truly mattered, and what was I willing to lose – and to keep? I had to turn inward and use the emotions as a portal to answer these existential questions. I learned about my primal fears, my emotional survival patterns, and how to work with the power of my instincts.

It's also worth mentioning that fear, regardless of what triggers it, is one of the primary causes of illness. Fear sets off the amygdala – the part of our brain responsible for fight or flight response, and that response shuts down our frontal lobe (thinking), our digestive system, and our immune system. And if the immune system is shut off, we're more susceptible to disease. Worry, anxiety, and stress keep our system in survival mode and prevent us from functioning at full physical, emotional, intellectual, and intuitive capacity. I don't say this to scare you; I say this to give you a vital piece of actionable information that empowers your physical, emotional, and mental wellness.

Strong, sudden emotions "make us irrational" because we're operating from the brain's survival mode – especially if we've had experiences that left deep emotional imprints or trauma. Because emotions anchor memories into the unconscious, we instinctively respond to situations and people that trigger those memories, often without thinking. This is why it's so important to bring mindful awareness to our emotions and noticing where they arise, in what situations, or around certain people so that we can understand what they are telling us and where the story originated.

When we bring that level of conscious awareness to emotions that have been hijacking our best efforts, we can then undertake the compassionate work of releasing the emotional charge and reprogramming the unconscious. We learn to work with our biology, and the biological nature of our emotions, instead of mindlessly rejecting our emotions as unwanted aspects of ourselves. The integration of emotions begins with understanding that they are part and parcel of who you are. Emotions exist to give you information through sensation, which can not only save your life but also tell you unequivocally when something is *right*.

How You Feel Influences What You Think

On an energetic level, thoughts are *electric*, and emotions are *magnetic*. Together, they create a unified field of experience through which we filter information and make sense of our world. If you think of an electric current, you might perceive it as going out into the world from its source. This is how thoughts work: they push out into the world as ideas, actions, and behaviors that catalyze and create our experience externally. Emotions, on the other hand, pull us inward. Emotions attract and magnetize experiences to us, and through our interpretations, we are given opportunities to choose differently depending on how we want to feel.

What it all boils down to is this: how you feel influences what you think. When our internal world holds a certain perspective (and magnetic charge), we inevitably see that reflected back to us in our interactions and experiences. When you change your perspective about something, everything else changes with it. Your emotions move your thoughts into tangible action and manifestation; thoughts give form to the impulse or urge arising inside you, as your body is responding to sensory data on a cellular level.

Thoughts and emotions work together and often are influenced in ways we don't perceive consciously. This is what can make them challenging to work with. Thoughts can evoke emotions and vice versa. Many of us don't realize just how we are prone to making emotional decisions. Even the most reasonable and logical people have blind spots and biases that make purely rational decision-making nearly impossible. It is not inherently bad or wrong to make decisions based on emotions – rather, it is *unexamined* emotional interference that negatively impacts our ability to reason.

What this means is that we must become familiar with our emotional range; the specific flavors of our diverse and nuanced emotions. We must become knowledgeable about how we feel so that we know when we are being influenced by our emotions and can factor that into our responses. This is a fundamental shift: from reacting to responding. It is critical to bring our conscious, objective awareness to the experience we are having rather than suppress it or stuff it down. This does not serve you, for emotions are messages that direct us to important (and sometimes painful) memories and internalized beliefs.

Emotions ground our thoughts and give them expression, intensity, and form. When I say emotions are magnetic, I am describing this experience. Emotions "glue" our thoughts together to form stories and experiences that become internalized beliefs over time if we are not aware. Emotions also draw our experiences deeper into the body, rooting them into our foundational scripts of selfhood. Here, buried far below the surface, they often become unconscious – that is, until we bring our awareness to what we are actually feeling. We can tell if we like an idea or not based on the emotions we experience. We might not always understand the "why" behind this feeling, but that's not the point of cultivating awareness.

We are becoming masters of the subtle. We don't always know logically why certain habits, programs or patterns surface in our lives, yet we can learn how to listen to what they reveal about us. Memory and emotions are intimately connected – and thus make it challenging to discern what is real and what is remembered. It's fair to say that we can't trust our memory – it is *not* fact.

Although we'd like to think that we recall things as they were, the reality is that memories fade and deteriorate over time. It has been shown in numerous studies that our memories disintegrate each time we recall them. Yet even if we don't remember a situation accurately, we are still able to connect to the emotions that were originally present. This is what we anchor to; how we felt about something, not what actually happened. The degree to which that memory affects you today is related to how strongly you feel about it. However, if you've worked through an emotional charge around a memory, you'll find it harder to retrieve – or that it's less of a big deal in retrospect. When the magnetic charge of emotion has been released, you no longer need to replay, relive, or recreate the memory.

How much of your conscious attention is given over to emotions that exist outside the present moment? When we ruminate on our emotions, we re-create the energetic experiences that went with them and magnetize the external ingredients to us through our energetic field. This is why rumination without action can be so harmful to our psyche – if we don't take a new action or let go, we don't complete the emotion. This leads to a sense of stuckness, and the inability to move forward, all while still experiencing the unwanted emotion. Emotions are data, information, and when processed correctly, can guide us to better informed decision making. This is no easy feat and it's not something we've been taught, so give yourself the benefit of compassion and understanding.

You can work with unprocessed memories and emotions that cause problems in your present life in many ways. One of the most effective is Eye Movement Desensitization and Reprocessing or EMDR, a form of integrative psychotherapy that uses eye movement, tones, or tapping to help "move" problem experiences out of your brain and replace them with new ones conducive to your wellbeing. You are no longer guided by negative emotions, feelings, and behaviors caused by unresolved experiences pushing you in the wrong direction. When you completely "digest" an experience in this way, you are left with appropriate emotions, understanding, and perspectives that lead to useful behaviors, interactions, and results in the present, and for the future.

Emotional Dysfunction Can Manifest as Depression

Distortion in our emotional field can make it challenging to discern what actions to take. There are many forms of distortion that are normalized: whether it is being told you are "too much" for expressing yourself authentically or made to feel that your emotions aren't valid. When we dismiss our experience or emotions as unimportant, we move into dangerous territory. We do this unconsciously, often due to childhood conditioning where we were "taught" that emotional expression was either bad, wrong, or came with unwelcome consequences. This idea was then reinforced by the world around us.

Oftentimes, it's not that we are afraid of our emotions, but we are unwilling to feel the discomfort they bring up. When I first started exploring the depths of my emotional center, it was because my world was being rocked and it felt like I had no other choice but to dive in and do the work. I was intuitively asking myself questions like, "Why do I feel this way?", "Where are these emotions coming from?" and "Why am I feeling these now?"

The beautiful storm that illuminated the subterranean layers underneath the surface of my mind hit every part of my life at once: I suddenly lost hearing in my left ear and my dog, Barrington, was diagnosed with cancer. This was shortly after I left a high-profile leadership role (which some called "career suicide") to launch my own business – and none of my efforts were working. My leap of faith was creating a cash-flow crunch while we were remodeling our home. Andrew and I were fighting, and our marriage was strained.

In the midst of this, I gave the public keynote where I shared vulnerable lessons I learned in my first marriage – namely, the suppressed emotions and intuitive hits I was getting that all pointed to one thing: the relationship wasn't right for me in the end. The talk I was in the process of preparing, while my current life was falling apart, revealed old pockets of shame, guilt, and grief hidden below the surface of my psyche.

I realized that I hadn't fully grieved the loss of my old self in my first marriage. On top of that, I was now confronted with all the feelings I didn't want to feel: heartbreak, the impending loss of a loved pet, fear of losing Andrew, fear of financial ruin, fear of failure, the sense that I was unsupported, and disappointment at how much hadn't worked out according to my expectations. I felt wounded and overwhelmed by all the things I was confronted with and because of that, I felt additional shame and self-judgment. It sounds dire and it felt that way. There were days where I felt like the victim of unseen forces; that I was being punished for choosing to follow my passions over convention. I thought at times that I had completely ruined my life and would never recover.

I couldn't see it in the moment, but I was in a deep process of letting go of emotional blockages and negative narratives that had been inside of me for years. I was still letting go of an old, false self as the new, true self came online. For several months, I was involved in deep healing work that I never knew I needed to do. I looked at all the times when I had felt shame and judgment towards myself. I finally started to acknowledge all the grief I was repressing. For a long time, I felt completely broken and at the bottom of my life. For the first time, I felt lost.

The depression that consumed me for a few months was a low point. I tried to power through it with old tactics. I drove myself harder to make things work with my mind, my logic, and sheer force of willpower. But any action that I attempted to take led to unsuccessful outcomes. I was constantly thwarted and frustrated. I didn't know what to do with all the emotions that came up, but through the process of directing my awareness, I started to learn practices that brought me back into connection with myself. It was only through the embodied process of letting go and integration that I started to understand how these emotions functioned and the dissonance they were illuminating within me. Here, I began to have compassion for myself. This allowed me to see how emotional dysfunction can manifest as depression. And, it allowed me to identify, acknowledge, and admit that my awakening was precipitated by burnout.

Burnout was officially recognized by the World Health Organization in 2019. Because our culture doesn't value emotional wellbeing in the same way that we value success, we often tend to overdraw our reserves of the former in search of the latter. Burnout tends to happen when we are taxing our emotional reserves rather than cultivating them in replenishing ways. Burnout in the professional world often manifests as a result of overextending ourselves without checking in with our needs and emotions first. This is easy to do if you are not connected with your emotional center. Feeling disconnected internally makes it harder to self-regulate and resource ourselves when we are riding emotional waves.

Relying on others to manage, mediate, or moderate our emotions is the opposite of a healthy loving relationship with ourselves. If you are always managing your emotions in order to fit into other people's definitions and ideas of who you are, it's going to feel harder to connect to your authentic self and honor what's true for you. This is called emotional labor. Learning to experience and release your emotions is an ongoing practice of cultivating self-efficacy. It might not always feel safe to express yourself in certain spaces; yet learning how to hold and honor your emotional experience will make it easier for you to navigate more difficult conversations with others.

Experiencing interpersonal stressors at work is recognized as one of the most threatening sources of stress. Not knowing how to navigate conflict with a colleague or communicate your needs clearly and effectively can turn a small tension into a source of ongoing exhaustion and physical depletion, depending on your ability to deal with external stressors. Diminishing your emotions suppresses your wellbeing, for they are deeply interconnected. Disharmony is the experience of feeling one way and operating in another, creating a rift between emotions and actions that amplifies the feeling of imbalance. Over time, if this isn't addressed it creates the conditions for more serious imbalances such as depression. Depression is the body's way of alerting you to a significant distortion that is interrupting your ability to effectively self-regulate in the way your system requires.

Right Relationship Leads to Better Outcomes

When you come into the right relationship with your emotions and learn to feel them in healthy ways, you inevitably start to lead your life with more conscious awareness. This practice creates opportunities for you to address imbalance at the root and take responsibility for the strategies that no longer serve your growth.

When you're not connected to your emotional center, it's easier to feel out of control in your life. This is often because we are not listening deeply to our emotional center. Our emotions are also often clouded by other people's stories, ideas, and judgments about who we are. It can be challenging to discern between those voices and our internal voice of authority, especially if we haven't built up the experience or wisdom to know the difference.

As I started to work with my emotions, I realized that many of my routine strategies were actually forms of numbing my pain. It was confusing at first because on the surface, I thought I had overcome my past and risen above my suffering. I counted on my resilience and determination as the reasons I was able to get back on my feet after leaving my first marriage to start my life anew. Working hard to achieve my professional goals had become a way to avoid the grief and heartbreak that were intricately woven into my selfhood.

I discovered this truth as I plumbed the depths of my emotional despair. Although I had originally stuffed these emotions away because they were too painful to deal with at the time, the unhealed trauma was now disrupting my life in larger ways. Certain people and situations were being magnetized to me by those unresolved emotions so that I would have another opportunity to feel them fully and gain the wisdom from the original, and repeating, lessons.

As I acknowledged each unexpressed and suppressed emotion, I had to go through an often-painful process of feeling what I hadn't allowed myself to feel before. This challenged my sense of identity and fortitude. I saw the ways my arrogance, naivete, and pride had driven many of the decisions that I felt victimized by. I had to feel this all, notice this all, and be with this all. It was the only way to let it go – and to allow the past, and all those emotions, to let *me* go.

After a while, I felt better: clearer, lighter, joyful. I began having spontaneous moments of bliss. Though they were short-lived, these transcendent experiences were proof that my emotional center was changing. My outer world began to change as well. Though more things fell out of my life, what and who remained was strong and aligned. Before long, different people and opportunities entered my life – all noticeably more aligned with my authentic self.

As a result of my inner work, my relationship with Andrew deepened and our marriage became a conscious container for our mutual growth. I was approached by my new business partners to join their company in a leadership role that leveraged all my best skills and passions. I met amazing women who quickly became part of my inner circle of most trusted sisters. I began to understand how to bring forward a deep, driving desire to share my story and wisdom to facilitate the awakening and growth of others. This book is one of those ways. All of this emerged from the destruction and despair once I faced my emotions with courage and compassion.

If you've ever wondered why the same kinds of "bad" people, jobs, relationships, or situations come into your life, know that this is not a coincidence; it's part of your path to self-mastery. Consider it your on-the-job training, for you have to feel your way through it. You have to be willing to acknowledge your emotions, observe your behaviors, identify your triggers, step away from your stories, detach from judgment. You have to be with the physical sensations in your body and emotional centers. You have to feel the feelings all the way so they can be released; complete.

Letting go is akin to clearing out emotional baggage trapped in your psyche, energy field, and body. Releasing the stuck emotions shifts your energetic frequency. You have more space (stillness) to receive the intuitive signals that are constantly flowing to and through you. What was once a jammed, scratchy signal is now a crystal-clear channel of grace and guidance.

All wounds are cellular memory patterns that block us from becoming healthy and whole. These keep us from expressing our full potential. This incongruity is what causes our suffering. Not healing yourself further suppresses those unhealthy patterns, creating more chronic conditions, and often leading to deeper layers of dis-ease in the body and mind. Attuning yourself allows you to recognize the symptoms of inner discord before they take a deeper root: apathy, grief, anger, fear, confusion, frustration, and pain all point to aspects of ourselves that need recognition and integration. To find inner authority we need to cultivate inner harmony. You must become your best advocate and ally in order to give voice to your inner authority.

Emotions Integrate the Self

We all have biases and blind spots that influence our understanding and perspective of reality. However, in order to harness the power of our emotions, we need to develop an awareness of when we are operating from this place. This increases our ability to respond from our sovereignty instead of defaulting to the ego's defense mechanisms and coping strategies.

Defense mechanisms serve a purpose; they are natural and normal. We use them to protect ourselves from difficult emotions like anxiety or guilt, when we feel threatened, or when we are overwhelmed by our feelings, undesirable thoughts, or painful memories. Though we banish certain memories, urges, or impulses to the unconscious, they don't disappear. Instead, they continue to exert a powerful influence on our behavior. So, we cope. Often, we project that unwanted, unconscious material onto others. Or, we repress, deny, or displace. Do you know your go-to defense mechanisms and coping strategies? Do you notice in what situations these kick in? Can you identify what emotions you're protecting yourself from?

A common experience people have is experiencing or relating to another's emotions as a reflection of their own. This can be projection (a coping mechanism) or projective identification (where we unconsciously place aspects of self, either good or bad, onto another person). Sometimes there is another mechanism at work here: empathy. You may have heard the term "empath" and understand it to mean someone who indiscriminately feels *everything*: their own feelings and emotions, as well as those of others, without the ability to "turn off." It doesn't sound like the kind of subtle superpower we'd want, as we already have our hands full with our own emotional processing. However, empathy is a vital component of relating and building mutually-beneficial, honest, loyal, and long-standing relationships.

Empathy is our ability to feel what someone else is feeling and to imagine what they might be going through. We are able to put ourselves in someone else's shoes from a multidimensional perspective, which offers us the gifts of deep understanding and compassion. There are different levels of empathy; generally higher in women, though many men find they are served by this as well. We must learn to discern when we're feeling deeply for someone else *and* taking that inside of ourselves. We can feel *for* another person's situation, but we can't feel their feelings *for them*. It's vital that we understand that distinction and set clear boundaries. Empathy is not sympathy. You can care about someone without taking on their emotions.

Get in the practice of asking yourself: What is mine? Are these feelings mine? The ability to recognize what emotions are actually yours versus the emotions or projections of another can help clarify where you need to take empowered action. Learning how to monitor and check in with your emotions allows you to make better decisions when you find yourself triggered or reactive.

Regulating your emotions isn't denying your reality but rather using it as an opportunity to reflect on what's true for you in the moment you feel something arising.

Rather than react from fear, you can use these triggers as the opportunity to have a conversation with yourself, check in, and re-align to address the issue. Emotional regulation gives you a powerful tool to work *with* your emotions rather than escaping entirely. Ultimately, we cannot suppress emotions indefinitely. Eventually, they come out, usually in a flood; the proverbial dam breaks, and we're swept away by a torrent of unfinished emotional business that takes us offline. Learning to regulate helps you tolerate the ups and downs within a reasonable window without denying your feelings or becoming overwhelmed. We learn to ride the waves, so to speak.

When you are in command of your emotional center, you become a more effective leader – someone who can relate to others because you know how to relate to yourself. You're not afraid to feel, to express, and to use emotional insights to make decisions. This new world we are living in requires that we as leaders are in touch with our emotions and that we are capable of attuning to those of others as well. Emotional intelligence and emotional regulation are skills that we must prioritize. Collaboration and communication are two key components of getting things done, and if we aren't approaching every interaction from a place of emotional integrity and wholeness, we won't be as effective or productive.

Emotions are subtle energetic waves and thus felt by others. If you are operating out of your integrity, your internal dissonance will impact those around you. Whether they (or you) realize it or not, they can feel it. These are the subtle signals that our intuition picks up, and that we unconsciously respond to. Yet when we work with our discomfort to transform difficult emotions, we build resilience and emotional intelligence within ourselves and inspire others to do the same.

Standing in your power means having the wherewithal to express feelings and emotions in a way that respects your boundaries and is respectful towards others.

When we don't own or express our emotional experience, it forces others to fill in their own blanks about what's going on when they feel that something is being communicated but not consciously addressed in the conversation. It can't surprise us when we are then "misunderstood"- we've left the door wide open for the other person to complete the story. As much as I'd like to say we can read minds, it's more appropriate to say we can read emotions, and those tell an altogether different narrative. Are you in control of your narrative?

Sometimes, I experience strong surges of emotion that "come out of nowhere." I've noticed this during times of collective anxiety such as 9/11 or the pandemic and ensuing protests and riots. I've also noticed it after a frustrating interaction with someone, after watching something disturbing or violent, or when working on personal things like writing, which require me to re-experience memories and their related emotional charges. Other times, I have no idea what hit me, but I know that it did. The moments I've had the presence of mind to communicate this, I have saved myself from unnecessary chaos. This has been most prevalent with Andrew, who is the most natural person to receive my displaced emotions.

We tend to take it out on those closest to us. In the moments when I am emotionally on edge, I tell Andrew, "I'm processing some big emotions right now and I'm not feeling great." This gives him the necessary information to *know* that whatever my mood or emotional state in that moment, it isn't directed at him and he can choose how to best respond. Even the simplicity of stating this helps to diffuse the unproductive emotions that threaten to take over. Instead, the overwhelm dies down a little. We need space to process. Sometimes it's a conversation. Sometimes it's a solo endeavor. It's never a battle.

One of the biggest hurdles to emotional integrity is overcoming the discomfort that many emotions naturally elicit. We avoid uncomfortable conversations because we don't want to deal with the emotions that are in us, or those of someone else. How many times have you decided not to speak up, stand your ground, call someone out, defend yourself, or demand what's right because you didn't want to deal with the awkward, uncomfortable feelings? Emotional discomfort often masquerades as fear. You're not afraid of the conversation, you're simply unwilling to have it. It's a choice. If we don't overcome this discomfort, we'll sit in anger, resentment, and victimhood instead of reaching resolution, clarity, and a path forward. We must have the courage to say what needs to be said, without attachment, blame, or projection. We must be ready to make clear statements about what we desire, what's going on, what's not working, and what we want to change. Most importantly, we need to practice listening to ourselves and others without judgment, expectation, or emotional reaction.

Time and again, the conversations that I expected to be the most awkward and difficult were always the most important ones. Even though they didn't always feel fun or easy, the resulting shift in my sense of personal power improved the relationship or situation for the better.

As the Black Lives Matter and social justice movement came forward in full force in 2020, we witnessed what systemic injustice looks like – some of us for the first time. I had so much to learn about systemic racism and why inequality exists in America. My privilege was uncomfortable to look at. As I did my research and listened to Black, Indigenous and People of Color (BIPOC) voices, I experienced denial, disbelief, and resistance. After that came the light of truth, deep understanding, and a fierce commitment to never staying silent again. What was even more uncomfortable, at first, was talking to people about it.

Two of my colleagues, including the CEO of our firm, are black men. One of our board members is a black woman. My approach to the conversations was, admittedly, a little bumbling at first. I was at a loss for words. I wanted to ask – how were they affected, how did they feel, were they okay? My colleagues were open about their experiences, thoughts, and feelings. My partner began his response with, "Don't take this the wrong way …" and expressed the challenge of suddenly receiving a barrage of texts, calls, and emails while trying to run the business during the height of the pandemic. Our board member, a veteran real-estate executive, told me that in her workplace, no one had asked or approached her about it. She generously and graciously told me (horror) stories of how she had to navigate constant discrimination in her professional life.

Even though I felt awkward and sheepish, I felt it was more important to be honest about my ignorance. My discomfort is a momentary drop in the ocean of suffering that too many people of color have been enduring for centuries. We can't affect change if we don't push against the very thing that keeps things the same – comfort, familiarity, and personal insulation from uncomfortable truths.

We can't know or assume what anyone else is feeling. We can only know what we are feeling and approach a conversation with that level of sovereignty. I am responsible for myself, and you are responsible for yourself. Your pain is not anyone else's problem. Blame keeps you stuck in victim consciousness. Taking ownership of your inner work is what builds self-mastery and sovereignty. There are benefits to experiencing all your emotions, even the unpleasant ones.

You'll find over time that when you honor your emotions, they will impart their wisdom and show you the way to work with them. As you feel the emotions, let them teach you their lessons. Let them show you where you stepped out of alignment or need to course correct. Let them alert you to the violation that happened. Let them speak the rage or the grief or the frustration they feel so you can cleanse them of their energetic charge. What is left after this process is the purity of your spaciousness. It is here that we can hear the divine within us speak.

Emotional regulation is not about discarding the emotions that don't feel good. We can, and must, approach emotions from a neutral place; neither seeking the good nor avoiding the bad. Treat it all as data. The connection between intuition and productivity is simple: you are no longer working against yourself. Rather, you are in flow and using the information available to you.

If you seek optimal performance, then you are seeking this state of consciousness. The flow state, also known as the peak performance state, emerges from a radical alteration in normal brain function. The clunky prefrontal cortex goes offline, along with its self-monitoring functions (second-guessing, self-doubting, the inner nag) that slow down decision-making. Flow states correlate to alpha and theta brain waves; the realms of boundless creativity and connection where learning is easy, and ideas combine in truly innovative ways. The body is flooded with the pleasure-inducing, performance-enhancing neurochemicals (the molecules of emotion): endorphins, norepinephrine, dopamine, anandamide, and serotonin, which enhance physical performance as well as "the three horsemen of rapid-fire problem-solving": attention, pattern recognition, and lateral thinking.

In flow states, we operate in a primal alignment that feels automatic and easy. In flow states, we operate in emotional alignment with higher frequencies that fuel motivation and feel good, often blissful. Our sense of self and time vanishes; we are "in the zone" or "in the pocket," feeling and performing at our best. We have access to subtle information to make instant, intuitive decisions in the moment, and we take action accordingly. Problem solving is nearly automatic and we act without hesitation. Ideas, imagination, and inspiration naturally follow, and the path forward is immediate and clear.

Reflection Questions:

1. What emotion(s) do I try to avoid? What triggers those emotions to come up? What techniques do I use to avoid it?

____

____

____

____

2. What emotion(s) do I want more of in my life? What triggers those emotions to come up? What can I do to increase my feel-good emotions?

____

____

____

____

3. What situations or conversations give me the most discomfort? What am I usually unwilling to talk about or express to others? What are my coping habits, escape hatches, distractions, and avoidance techniques?

____

____

____

____

Actionable Practices:

1. Begin to practice "emotional noticing," a powerful self-mastery practice.

   a. Can you bring awareness to the emotion, and the thoughts that go with it?

   ____

   ____

   ____

   ____

   b. Where in your body does the emotion originate?

   ____

   ____

   ____

   ____

   c. What behaviors are triggered? What do you do? What regularly happens?

   ____

   ____

   ____

   ____

d. Can you interrupt the process when you notice the unconscious pattern playing out?

____

____

____

____

e. What happens when you make even a small change in your reaction? How do you feel?

____

____

____

____

2. Working with your Defining Moment again, journal the answers to these questions:

a. What did I feel then?

____

____

____

____

b. Can I identify what emotions were most present for me then?

____

____

____

c. Can I identify what caused those emotions to arise and what information they contained (outside of a narrative)?

d. Can I discern today what my emotions were trying to tell me then? Does this change my experience/ memory and my understanding now?

3. Letting Go technique for working with powerful emotions:

a. When a powerful emotion rises within you, allow it to come up. Don't resist it. Let it run its course through you. This may take time, so stay with it. Don't judge the emotion and notice any thoughts that come up – and let those fall away. Try to focus on the energy of the emotion and where it arises in your body, and let the energy out. Notice if you want to vent, do something physical, eat, or any other distraction or numbing technique. Stay with it. Notice the resistance when it comes up, and surrender any attempts to modify how you feel or what is happening. Stay in open-minded, open-hearted curiosity. Allow the energy to flow, and eventually, it will change or lessen. When you begin to feel lighter, you'll notice that there is less of an energetic charge.

137

Go Deeper:

1. *Molecules of Emotion: The Science Behind Mind-Body Medicine* by Dr. Candice Pert

2. *Permission to Feel. Unlocking the Power of Emotions to Help Our Kids, Ourselves, and Our Society Thrive* by Marc Brackett

3. *Letting Go* by David R. Hawkins

CHAPTER 5

Wisdom of the Body

Mantra:

I am home in my body. I trust my instincts.

I am grateful to be alive.

My body is a temple of transcendent intelligence.

I give my body permission to be exactly as it is.

I give myself permission to listen to my body.

I give myself permission to care for and love my body.

Keywords:

Body, Earth, Matter, Mass, Substance,

Solidity, Strength, Foundation, Vessel

The body is one of the most important aspects of developing inner authority, for our body is the container of our essence. Here, the alchemy of spirit occurs. Our ideas and emotions are rooted here, as is our energy source. The word human comes from Humus, the soil from which all things grow. The body is the vessel that connects us to the Earth and to life itself, thus it is a critical place to anchor your awareness of all that you experience.

Your body is a conduit for intuition. The physical sensations and signals that your body sends communicate important messages from your transcendent intelligence centers. In other words, you don't have intuition, you are intuitive. The esoteric mind and emotional realm often feel conceptual and elusive; whereas the physical expressions of intuition are often easier to identify and understand because we can bring our awareness and attention to what the body is saying. As you tune into the body, you begin to cultivate a new level of trust in yourself.

When you learn to trust your body, you naturally cultivate more confidence, empowered action, and a feeling of being in control. While you are *not* "just a body," self-mastery and sovereignty are not possible without it! The body is your inner authority expressed and anchored in physical form. This is why your body is beautiful: because it is the container for *you.*

Operating within your intuition is easier than you might imagine. We've all had numerous moments of intuitive knowing. We've all said, "I have a good/bad feeling about this..." at some point or another. Now, where does *that* knowing come from? How do we know we know? Where does that sensation, that feeling in the body, come from? And, how can we learn to actively work with our intuitive feelings and integrate them within our life and work?

Your gut-brain is ground zero for your intuitive knowing. This is the most important area of the body where we *feel* our intuition working away. There is a good reason for saying that we have a "gut feeling," or that we should "trust our 'gut' " and it is all part of our incredible biology. The gut is called the enteric nervous system (ENS) and, due to the extent and degree of its autonomy, the ENS is considered by biologists as a bona fide second brain. The network of neurons in the gut is as vast and complex as the neural system in our spinal cord. The gut brain can also operate independently of both the cerebral brain and the central nervous system, so when you feel an answer in your gut, don't wait for your intellect to catch up. With that much brain power, your gut can think for itself. The question is: are you listening?

The fear signals that you receive in your gut when something feels off is your primal response to real or perceived danger – and it's usually right. It always occurs before your brain, your ego, your thoughts, your memories, or your programming can give you their distorted opinion. The gut is the home of pure, unadulterated primal knowing. Your gut-brain also gives out "yes" signals that can help us interpret our energy levels and pleasure sensations. Translating this subtle language and learning how to use it effectively alongside your intellect can help you unpack, process, and put into action a whole world of meaning.

The Ground of Your Future Self

When you shift your energetic state, you are supporting an alchemical process of releasing old stories, programming, and memories that no longer serve you. All movement energetically and emotionally is metabolized by the body, so your physical state actually becomes the *ground* for your future self.

Put simply, when you bring attention, intention, and action towards the desired change, you start to cultivate a deeper awareness of the conditions that sustain it. Think of the body as a multidimensional radio transmitter, constantly receiving and producing invisible frequencies that are interpreted through the biological system itself. Our job is to be in our conscious awareness, trust what the body is saying, and take action on its intel.

With the increased awareness you are developing, you are empowering yourself with the techniques and modalities that will allow you to read your bodily signals with more accuracy and speed, becoming much more efficient at understanding your needs and responding in alignment.

As the body shifts in frequency, the physical matter changes as well. You might find yourself feeling lighter or enjoying more clarity and focus. You might feel more resonant with your experiences and that life is flowing more easily. This is because the work you have been doing is deeply interconnected across the body's biological systems in addition to the mental and emotional ones. The body is a complex biological machine comprising a multitude of systems, many with their own "brains," operating as a cohesive network. Only the ego operates as the singular, separatist "I" – the lone wolf attempting to command-and-control a perfectly designed collaborative evolutionary system that we inhabit with limited, but ever-increasing consciousness.

Enlightenment is exactly what it sounds like: releasing the heavy density of past stories so that our bodies respond vibrationally with increased vibrancy, energy, and health. As you go through the catharsis of releasing old concepts and integrating the learnings of your past experiences and former selves, you start to be more present in your body now. You might start to feel something you haven't felt before; the desire to be *here*, present, in your authentic fullness and authority. As you create space for new situations and let go of ones that no longer serve you, you will inevitably start to feel more grateful for what is, more loving of who you are, and more accepting of where you are. Your natural state of grace reveals itself in the glow of your being.

Bliss is your birthright. The science doesn't lie: we're literally hard-wired for pleasure. When you ask your body, it will tell you that it too prefers a state of balance, harmony, and happiness in order to function at optimal levels.

Intuition Speaks Through the Body

Our intuition is vastly more intelligent than the conscious mind or the intellect. Ironically, we rarely give it precedence when determining what is true for us. Many people haven't developed a deep relationship with their bodies – and when this happens, it can be difficult to know exactly what it is saying when it speaks to us. Even worse, you might ignore, deny, or silence the intuitive voice when it comes through. The body senses what the mind won't speak of, and it's not shy about letting us know.

I've learned this the hard way many times: staying in the wrong relationship for too long, losing my life savings to investment fraud, letting others' expectations dictate my goals and squash my dreams, and pushing myself so hard to succeed that I burnt out. In each situation, my body was giving me clear signals that I consistently ignored. Yet when I learned to listen to my body's intuition, I began feeling more safe and secure in my decisions and my self-efficacy. I started to see the results I wanted, often without even trying. It took me some time to build the muscle of trust, but when I did miracles emerged in my everyday: I found the best possible business partners, my podcast pivoted into my passion of helping others learn about building their healthy financial foundations, and I'm working with my dream publishing team to bring my book to life. I'll expand more on the coherence that brought these dreams forward in a later chapter, but for now, it is enough to say that the body operates as a manifestation device, so to speak, for ultimately it expresses what we believe to be true.

There are stories from all corners and walks of life demonstrating the validity of intuitive responses. From military strategists to global business leaders to innovative visionaries, we are starting to see a shift in the way we talk about intuition in professional spaces. We are surrounded by stories that demonstrate a causal response between the gut-brain and our intuition.

For instance, when Bob Lutz, then-President of Chrysler, was asked how he had the insight for the Dodge Viper – a massively successful car that turned the ailing company around – he said: "It was a visceral feeling – and it just felt *right*."

Richard Branson, the renowned founder of the Virgin brands, is famous for trusting his instinct and intuition when it comes to making key business decisions – such as launching Virgin Airlines.

Kevin Systrom, the founder of Instagram said, "I do distinctly remember, when we were deciding what to do, I had this moment where I really *felt* clarity; that the fact that phones now had cameras meant there was going to be this massive shift in how people shared their lives."

The body *makes sense* – literally. Its signals and sensations are tangible: we can feel, touch, and know what is there. We recognize our body as ours, even if we haven't developed a real relationship with it. It's the most accessible place for us to begin accessing the more intangible realms of our unconscious. The body is intuitive, even if you don't feel that you have access to your intuition.

Your body is constantly sensing, storing, processing, and relaying information to different parts of your system so that you can continue to stay alive. Talk about an ally! Have you ever stopped to ask what intelligence is running all these functions or how that's possible? Asking big questions like this places our attention on the miracle of the body we are in. We gain perspective and appreciation for just how much we don't know and how much we're already trusting this body with our life. Now we need to move into trusting the intuitive signals that the body is sending us on a daily basis to optimize our life and achieve our deep, driving desires.

Take a moment right now to think about a time that your intuition spoke to you through your body. Where do you get your "hits"? What do your "pings" feel like? Do you notice it in your gut? Does your eye twitch? Maybe you feel heat in your hands? Do you hear tone shifts in your inner ear? Do you feel a rush of energy through your spine? There are myriad ways that intuition communicates through the body, feelings, and physical sensations. These are all cues and clues that, with practice, we can attune to, learn to recognize, and act upon with confidence.

Intuition functions differently than our emotions do, for it almost always comes forth as a knowing: an aha moment, a download of perfect information, a flash of insight or answer out of nowhere, a premonition, an impulse to do something differently. Research shows compelling evidence that the body's perceptual apparatus is continuously scanning the future, a key to intuitive insight. The body is collecting and filtering data at a rate of 11 million bits per second, while the conscious mind only processes a fraction of that −50 bits per second. This means that in order to effectively synthesize such complexity, the body is drawing upon every cell, every organ, and every system to efficiently process this information. And all that information is available through our transcendent intelligence centers and intuitive signaling. The question is always – do we trust it, and will we heed it?

Your 'Other' Body

All matter is energy and energy is constantly moving. This is what creates electricity: the movement and activity of tiny quantum particles that we can't see. Every single object, from a particle of dust floating in space to a massive galaxy, has an electromagnetic frequency that influences and interacts with other things. We have a measurable electromagnetic field that extends far beyond the physical boundary of the skin. Thoughts have an electromagnetic frequency. Emotions have an electromagnetic frequency. Our bodies pick up on these subtle energetic cues.

The energetic body is the most esoteric and the least understood framework in the Western world. Like intuition, the idea of an energetic body has previously been dismissed as unscientific. However, advances in quantum science prove otherwise – from entanglement to dark matter, every object is quite alive; always in motion, never at rest, and interacting with other energy fields. Energy is inherent in everything, and we are no different.

Many ancient cultures knew about, acknowledged, and cultivated the energetic "body," which has been described in a myriad of ways. The ancient Egyptians called it the Ka. Eastern philosophies and practices that honor *chi* are working with the energy systems and meridians of the body. The great enlightened yogis talk of *chakras*, the energy centers of the body, and *prana*, the flow of breath that connects us to life itself.

You may have already sensed this "other" body existing within your physical one. Energetic sensitivity is a skill you can cultivate over time. With practice, you can learn to feel into and attune to your energy body. Notice when your energy is high or low. What situations drain you? How do you feel around different people? What experiences nourish you and make you feel more alive? Can you place attention on your energetic life force? What does it feel like? Does it have a color, a texture, or other imprint that you can recognize? Place attention on a particular part of your body – what do you sense?

There is a connection between organs, emotions, biological functions, and energy centers within the body. These energy centers correspond to the seven chakras in the body. Each of these centers vibrates at a specific frequency, responds to certain tones, and has an associated color (a frequency on the light spectrum) and corresponding pressure points. Acupressure, acupuncture, massage, and sound healing (such as the use of tuning forks and bowls), and color therapy are examples of non-medicinal modalities that take a holistic approach to healing physical ailments by taking into consideration the subtle aspects of the body systems.

Working with energy takes your intuition to a whole new level. Attuning to subtle, imperceptible sensations refines your awareness of more than just your physical existence; you cultivate an awareness of your place within the inevitable unfolding of evolution. Your connection to all things isn't an accident and while it may be mysterious to the rational mind, it makes perfect sense to your transcendent intelligence.

Let's Get Physical

Conscious awareness is a powerful function that we can harness when working with our mind and our emotions. Likewise, we can place our conscious attention on what's going on around us *and* inside of us. Paying attention to the body wakes up a vast world of information and answers that are available to us. By tuning into the subtle sensations that are present, you can start to notice how your physical form expresses itself to you.

Nowhere was this principle more evident to me than when I began to practice yoga. At first, my purpose for doing yoga was to reap the benefits of a strong physical practice that promised to reshape my body. Power yoga was particularly appealing, as I had a lot of energy to burn and a body that responds well to strong exercise. I thought I was going to gain more tone and strength; instead, I gained an intimate relationship with my body, my emotions, my mind, and my soul.

On the mat, I worked so much more than my muscles or my flexibility. With every posture, I was connecting breath to movement. I was opening pathways – from detoxifying the lymphatic system to calming the nervous system to carving new neural networks. I created space in my body and my mind. I could see my life with more clarity and feel what was right for me. For the first time in years, I was starting to trust myself. It was through mindful movement that I began to work more closely with the wisdom of my body and to unravel physical, emotional, and energetic knots. It was with yoga that I began healing the complicated relationship I had with my body.

The ancient yogis mapped out the relationship between the body, emotions, mind, and spirit. They understood the various centers of intelligence and the channel through which transcendent intelligence communicates with us. They knew, long before psychologists, neurobiologists or quantum physicists could prove it, that we are bio-energetic beings with incredible (if often dormant) potential.

If you've practiced yoga, you may be familiar with the sensation of relaxed satisfaction after class; an inner glow that speaks to both deep work and deep rest. What you feel is the physical connection to *all* parts of you. You are feeling the sensation of having brought these elements together in harmony, even if only for a short time. We call that coherence. However, the effects of yoga on your wellbeing are permanent. Once you begin to access the transcendent through the body, you've effectively opened a door to a new level of knowing. Your being serves as proof that you are stronger, deeper, broader, and more infinite than what you believe yourself to be.

You don't have to do yoga to understand this connection. Yoga isn't better than weightlifting – and, for the record, I do both! Any physical practice of movement or exercise, whether it's yoga, tai-chi, qigong, going to the gym, running, cycling, or dancing, it is simply a practice of intentionally connecting with the body as it moves. By placing attention on the body during movement, we enter into a different place – almost another world. This state of being is far removed from external distractions, old hurts, or the chatter of thoughts. Attention is focused, which brings you into immediate presence. Runners experience states of bliss, dancers experience joy and freedom, and many people who do any form of dedicated exercise say they feel more connected to a deep current within themselves, to a part they can't access other than through their own body, in movement, as One.

How often do you pay attention to the way you move your body? Do you bring attention to feel your body or parts of it? Do you exercise or have a physical practice? If so, do you do it mindfully or are you going through the motions to burn calories or hit other goals? If you don't like to or can't exercise, I invite you to try one of my favorite and simplest forms of mindful movement: walking.

Every body is unique and expresses itself differently. The body you find yourself in exists to help you experience the physical world through sensation and movement. The more you learn to move with your body and to explore its sensemaking intelligence, the more you'll discover the infinite possibility of what it can do, and what it can teach you.

Inner Body Awareness

Accessing your body's intuition doesn't need to be hard work. Neither does it require any additional actions on your part if you are simply willing to increase your level of awareness. Becoming adept in your body's subtle language is the only requirement. Checking in with yourself can be done at any moment – and the more you do it, the easier it becomes.

There is a name for the type of awareness you need to develop in order to connect to your intuitive signals: *interoception.* Interoception is inner body awareness, and cultivating this practice helps you become more intimately aware of, and familiar with, all your internal states: mental, emotional, and physical. Emotions naturally show up in the body and many of us have experienced them overtake us; losing our authority as we are dragged, pushed, and pulled by invisible forces. As we discussed in the previous chapter, learning to work with our emotions helps us to identify their purpose and message.

The body is here to help you process those emotions. Building a practice of interoception allows you to anchor your awareness inside yourself, creating steadiness amidst emotional storms. You'll begin to notice how your body responds and reacts to different situations. More importantly, you'll be better able to discern when you are feeling your own emotions in the moment, past emotions tied to old narratives or programming, other people's emotions, or external energies. Can you identify where in your body your emotions originate? Do they have a color, texture, or temperature? What physical sensations can you identify in moments of distress?

For example, during times of collective crises, we feel a heightened sense of anxiety, which can cause physical sensations like heart palpitations, stomach aches, gut issues, insomnia, depression, and a loss of physical energy. That anxiety is a response to the collective energy; to thousands or millions of people simultaneously feeling anxiety. Our bodies pick that up, we *feel* it, and we unconsciously internalize it.

With dedicated awareness, we can easily learn to work with our bodies and practice discernment in moments of apparent distress. What is subtle has a tangible impact, so working with it makes you a master of the subtle. You empower yourself through conscious responses to that which may have previously felt like an invisible enemy. Developing interoception and choosing conscious responses to external and internal stimuli serves to connect to your inner authority and further strengthen your self-mastery.

The Fertile Ground for True Sovereignty

Awareness in all its forms is the foundational principle behind personal development philosophies and practices. Agency begins with our awareness of the subtle, sensory, body-based feelings that permeate our experience. Knowing *what* we feel is the first step to uncovering *why* we feel that way.

We want to become adept at understanding what the body is telling us. This requires getting still, quieting the mind, and centering ourselves. This brings us into immediate presence within the body, where we can finally hear our intuition speak. You might have heard the phrase "getting into your body" and wondered what that actually means – after all, you use your body every day! How could you not be connected to it?

Perhaps you'll recognize yourself in this description. I was unconsciously (yet purposely) disconnecting from my body through always keeping busy, being on-the-go, crossing things off my list, adding to my list, projecting into the future, and often ruminating on the past. I was constantly thinking about what worked and what wasn't working, what he said or she said, what others expected of me and where I wanted to be. I was always distracted by the next thing that wanted my attention.

Other ways we hide from our body include: over-thinking, distractions like sex, food, drugs, social media, and TV. Even exercise, especially over-exercising, obsessive dieting, and body dysmorphia are ways we disconnect from our bodies. We also disconnect from physical sensations and signals by projecting our emotions onto others instead of feeling and integrating them, trying to make ourselves disappear through numbing habits and behaviors, making ourselves small or minimizing needs...the list goes on.

Ask yourself: In what ways do I disassociate from my body? What am I trying to hide / escape / avoid? What do I tell my body and how do I treat it? Do I love my body? Do I even like being *in* my body?

Yet it is not just the physical presence of our body that matters but our ability to listen to what it needs.

The signals are subtle – aches and pains, the knowings we receive from our gut – until they are not. When we do not address the signals that the body is giving us through the expression and emergence of symptoms, we create the conditions for illness to manifest on deeper levels. This is referred to as dis-ease.

One of the most obvious expressions of dis-ease in the body is burnout: fatigue and chronic exhaustion, constant anxiety, and other stressors can push your system to the edge. Overwork, poor nutrition, lack of exercise, and lack of sleep also contribute to the body feeling stretched to capacity. We push ourselves and then punish ourselves for not going harder, faster, longer. Instead of relating to our body as an ally, we treat it as a commodity.

Most of us, especially women, have a dysfunctional relationship with our bodies. Our culture does not emphasize a holistic perspective of wellness but rather a capitalistic profiteering of perfection. We stop thinking about balance and get stuck thinking only in terms of the body's shape and size, grounding our focus in a narcissistic pursuit of superficial ideals.

You won't have a relationship with your body if you are not willing to relate to it in ways that feel loving, accepting, and understanding. Emphasizing ideal outcomes over ongoing connection with our physical vessel creates the conditions for self-loathing. After all – if you don't feel safe in your skin, how can you care for it? This conditioned detachment from our bodies as sacred and intelligent interconnected systems creates a division that deeply impacts our overall wellbeing. When I developed anorexia in my 20's, it was because I didn't want to be in my body – so instead, I punished it. Twenty years later, I'm still working on healing the relationship with my body. The path to wholeness and harmony begins with gratitude for the powerful, graceful, miraculous vessel that carries, protects, and allows the experience of life to be tangible.

Your body is not broken. Your body is not flawed. Your body is not ugly. Your body is literally *here for you.* Your body loves you – even when it's in pain, when it's old, when it's imperfect. Your body is the ground for all your deepest transformation and the home of your inner authority, for nothing is possible without it. Know that even if you have trauma, even if you feel shame and especially if you feel like you're past "fixing" – nothing is wrong with you. The more you come back to believing in the power of your body, the more you will start to realize true safety in your experience. This is the foundation of true sovereignty.

I wouldn't dare to presume that I can speak to what you've been through. It's never been my prerogative to tell anyone what to do, for I can't provide you with your answers and I can't walk in your shoes. I can only speak from my experience and what I found to be true for me: the more I tried to love my body as it was – not as I wished it to be – the more my whole world started to shift. My ability to manifest grew more powerful. I felt more in control of the circumstances and challenges I encountered along the way. The stronger I felt, the stronger my body got. As I became stronger, the more I wanted to care for my body rather than change it. Where before I had become embedded in a negative perspective, I was now cultivating a positive cycle of embodied power.

Cultivating Your Life Force

Our world is spinning fast. Change is happening at an exponential rate and many people feel disoriented by the disruption rapidly re-shaping our world. The internet gives us access to multiple streams of competing information all wanting to grab our attention for the wrong reasons. All this constant information coming in overloads our receptors and creates stress in the body as we try to regulate and respond.

In an era where we are constantly influenced by technology, it's critical to take care of your body, for it is doing the hard work of digesting all the data. Our environment is also filled with more harmful toxins and energetic pollutants that disturb the natural rhythms of our systems in ways that are often invisible until it's too late. If our bodies are not strong enough to manage the external impacts of our busy lives, then we are going to have a harder time resourcing our energy when we experience emotional or mental stress, or are taking the next big leap.

Anytime you level up in life, you draw on your reservoirs of energy: the strength and clarity necessary to navigate the unknown. Think of how you might prepare for a long race: you train, you build muscle, you hydrate. You practice diligently. You rest in between workouts so your body has time to repair itself before it must endure the next sprint. It's the same if you are starting a project, launching a business, or entering into a new relationship: each one of these situations will require an investment of time and energy. If you are depleted from the beginning, you won't be able to sustain yourself over the long run.

Your body is your responsibility. For some of us, that might feel like a punishment at first. It takes time to cultivate a loving relationship with the body if you have been conditioned to believe and act otherwise. Repairing the body in order to bring yourself to a healthy baseline is part of the reconciliation process. This is not to be conflated with a number on a scale. Rather, the repair is accomplished with simple, small steps: emphasizing life-giving food, taking time each day to move and connect with yourself, getting enough sleep, playing and having fun, engaging in creative pursuits or projects, and giving yourself rest, recovery and relaxation.

For a culture so disconnected from the body as a whole, we definitely love to talk about self-care. We are *sold* self-care constantly. In fact, it became "performative wellness," which caused even more stress when we thought we needed to add self-care to our already endless to-do lists. Don't get confused by influencers hawking the next wellness tea over social media – capitalism is not the answer here. Self-care can look like a lot of things, depending on your individual needs in the moment and it's often far simpler than you imagine. Sometimes it's turning off your phone, taking a walk, or taking a few deep breaths. If you want to release difficult emotions, for instance, self-care might be: screaming into a pillow, having a good cry in the bathtub, or indulging in a sensory massage. Self-care is not about shopping for something to make you feel good; it's taking responsibility to care for *your entire self*. You might be surprised by what self-care looks like for you.

The most important reason to take care of yourself? You cannot function at your highest capacity unless you are healthy and present in your body. Our energy is a function of our full aliveness, and if we are abusing ourselves, we are going to see that expressed in our physical container. You are not *just* your body: you are the caretaker of a sacred container that holds your true essence.

Refining Your Connection

As you develop an intentional, loving relationship with your body, working symbiotically with it to transmute old patterns, stuck emotions, past pain, and cellular disease, you will find that the more you clear, the more you feel. As you release energetic density, you discover inner authority's confident light.

I recommend the following core focus areas to further refine your connection with your body for a stronger flow of intuition: breath, nutrition, and rest.

The quickest, easiest, and most powerful practice for connecting to the body is breathing. There are countless benefits of mindful breathing– reducing stress, calming a frayed mind, strengthening the heart and lungs, improving blood circulation, detoxifying the lymph, increasing inner heat, and replenishing energy. Deep breathing clears toxins and feeds the body with life-giving, energizing oxygen, whereas shallow breathing accumulates toxins in the body which can lead to the development of illness over time. The beauty of this simple and potent practice is that we have full agency when it comes to breathing. Unlike other bodily functions that we cannot consciously control, we can choose how we want to breathe. There are many practices and forms of breathwork to explore: holotropic, kundalini, and pranayama breathing techniques, alternate nostril breath, or the box breath used by the Navy Seals. The core principle of both yoga and meditation involve a focus on the breath for good reason: the breath is our connection to our lifeforce and when we focus on it, we enter into communion with our transcendent self.

When I was 16, I was diagnosed with acute Crohn's Disease, a debilitating, chronic auto-immune disorder that affects the small intestine. My life changed almost overnight and I learned the vital role that food plays in treating and preventing illness. Nutrition is not what's listed on a label; nutrition is a responsibility to ensure my body's health and wellbeing over time. Food and nutrition are complex topics fraught with misinformation, political lobbying, and money-grabbing fads, many of which I've both followed and unraveled. Over the decades, I've seen much truth come to light, but none more important than this: every single person has unique nutritional needs and each of us is wholly responsible for the body we're in. In the same way, we have agency to consciously breathe and use the breath to enhance our wellbeing, so too do we have agency to understand what foods are helpful or harmful to our bodies, and to choose the most nourishing ones we can.

DNA testing can be a good starting point for understanding your body's unique needs and making informed decisions about what is actually good for you – from foods, to macros, to supplements. Ayurveda and Traditional Chinese Medicine are ancient practices that focus on holistic healing of the mind and the body, and most eastern and indigenous medicine deeply understands and works with plants to facilitate healing and maintain optimal health. Functional medicine is a modern Western approach to holistic health. But nothing is more important than your ability to listen to your body's needs and adjust accordingly. Crohn's Disease is considered incurable and requires ongoing pharmaceutical management – yet I haven't needed medication for over 15 years. Nutrition is how we sustain the body. Food can be poison or it can be medicine. The choice is yours.

The body has incredible regenerative powers, but it needs the right conditions to heal, grow, and evolve. Rest and sleep are fundamental aspects of good health on every level. The idea of stillness in any form is the antithesis to the modern culture of "always on:" working, striving, achieving, and producing. So many of us don't know how to rest, nor do we appreciate its essential importance. How many of us have a false belief that rest is bad – that it means you're lazy and will never achieve your goals or dreams? I grew up with this belief and I *still* struggle to slow down and fully rest.

With so much hero-worship around the mythology of what makes a successful entrepreneur or executive, no wonder most of us never seem to stop working. But ask anyone who has performed this way for any period of time, and they'll tell you it is unsustainable; something must give, and it's usually the body. It feels *good* to rest because it is. And if we take our mind, with all those negative thoughts out of the equation, we intuitively understand that it is necessary to do so. Rest refreshes, resets, and re-energizes the entire system. The body cannot always be on; it's unnatural and destructive. We can learn from athletes, who understand the need for rest and how it helps them perform better and achieve their most daunting goals.

Sleep has recently become an important topic of conversation in many circles, including those of performance enhancement. Dr. Matthew Walker, a neuroscientist and sleep expert who lectures on the importance of sleep and dreaming, has made a compelling case for why good quality and sufficient quantity of sleep is critical for optimal physical and cognitive performance, and how that is especially important in business. Sleep – and specifically dreaming – brings us in contact with some of our unconscious aspects of the self. Creativity and subtle connections are enhanced in a dream state, while the body repairs everything from nerve cells to brain tissue to the lining of the heart and intestines. Health is more than an active, intentional activity. Sometimes we have to give over this false sense of control and allow ourselves to be guided by the innate wisdom and intelligence of a body that never ceases to work for our highest potential and functioning.

Intuition Is Never Wrong

The body is a big transponder that gives intuitive signals through all that it is perceiving and processing. So let's say when you meet someone, and you get an immediate, instinctive bad feeling – that's your intuition. It's important to remember that once you get that "hit," your conscious mind will kick in and start to muddy the signal. It'll start to apply all kinds of filters and reasoning, run through programming, experiences, memories, thoughts, biases, narratives, and unprocessed emotional material. It reverts to the more efficient re-run rather than attempting to engage in a new thought pattern that requires more work. Remember, the unconscious is highly efficient because it runs on *existing* programming. All this happens in nanoseconds. If you're not sensitized to your intuitive signals, it's easy to ignore it, brush it off, and let the mind continue to go for what "you" prefer and what you unconsciously believe, even if you don't realize that it is something that might hurt you.

I can take my experience of investment fraud many years ago. My ego had an agenda and my mind was full of biases. It preferred an outcome that promised outstanding returns. I sunk my life savings into the investment even though I had a strong intuition that said: "This is not a good idea." I did not want to believe that anything bad could happen to me – I was smart, informed, and objective. I *wanted* to believe that I had made a good investment and allowed my own story to run away with me.

I rationalized away my concerns. When I reflect on what my body was telling me then, I feel it as a constricting energy field squeezing my head, followed by a sinking stomach and heightened anxiety and defensiveness. It was a "Code Red" kind of feeling and yet I kept going. I intuitively sensed this was not a good situation or person, but I kept justifying all the reasons why I didn't want to listen. In the end, it turned out to be a scam and I lost all my money.

This is the most obvious example I can provide about how the ego uses the logic of the mind and co-opts emotions to play out unconscious programs. My instinct was right. My intuition was right. And even though I could make the numbers work, there was always that nagging sense that this wasn't going to pay off in the way I intended.

I've been able to apply the wisdom gained from the fraud to the way I do business, evaluate investments, and make all my important decisions. I never question my gut now and always question the facts. We must always undertake this two-part process of doing both a fact-check and a gut-check. Both are important and necessary, and they work in tandem. What this means is that when you are evaluating anything – whether that's a new role, a project you want to take on, a business you want to start, a partner you are considering, and of course an investment opportunity or any large purchase, you must employ the dual process of the gut-check and the fact-check.

The fact-check is about obtaining the information and analyzing the data. Do the numbers make sense? Is it logical? Do the facts in the story line up? Perform background checks, do your research, ask the questions, map it out. Remove emotional responses and wishful thinking. The fact-check is all about the linear and logical functions of understanding whether the facts, data, and information check out.

The gut-check is where you pay close attention to your intuition. Notice the subtle signals in your body, especially your gut. When you're doing the fact-check, are you getting a funny feeling? Does something seem elusive, but you can't put your mental finger on it? When speaking to the person or people involved, how do you feel? What are your energy levels? How is your body responding? The gut-check is all about the subtle, intuitive signals and whether you're getting a yes. And if it isn't a strong yes; if there's even a hint of your intuition sending doubt, then it's a no.

You can have the perfect deal or the ideal outcome, even make the numbers say what you want them to say, but you can't change the person you're going to do business with. You can't change the signals you receive or what your gut tells you. You can ignore it at your own risk, for intuition is never wrong.

Manifest the Life You Desire

We can't get what we want if we don't take action to get it. Opportunities might come our way and occasionally strokes of luck happen – but if we aren't putting out the energy, nothing comes our way. This is why the body is so important: it takes ideas and inspiration generated by the mind and makes them into something real. This is all manifestation really is – bringing our internal experience, inspirations, and aspirations into externalized form.

Wishful thinking is just that – a thought –intangible and potentially deceptive. Research shows that our brains often cannot tell the difference between a wishful thought and a real outcome thanks to the release of neurochemicals. Saying we did something feels as good as doing it. We need to be very aware of this mechanism because it can keep us complacent and feeling good but without tangible results which, in the long run, contribute to feeling unsuccessful and ungrounded. We can use this same mechanism to our advantage: using active imagination and productive visualization to instill a new state of being and bring a vision to life. However, we must take steps toward the change we've identified as critical to our growth. Until we do, we stay stuck in obsession, fantasy, and escapism. To relate this to the chakra system, you could say we stay stuck in the 6th chakra – the third eye center.

You have more power than you realize. Intuition becomes productive when an opportunity is identified, and action is initiated. Nothing becomes real without us. We must ground the inspiration, vision, and enthusiasm into form. We must move that energy through the 1st chakra – the root – our connection to the Earth, matter, and form. In other words, we have to do something about it and make it real. That's what manifestation is all about. It's not wishful thinking. It's action-oriented. What that means is that you must acknowledge and honor the body as the vehicle that gives you expression in the world. It deserves our attention and respect, for fear is nonexistent when we're anchored in trust.

The mind-body connection is infinitely capable of creating whatever we want. Your body is basically a supercomputer that reinvents itself neurologically based on what you believe. Dr. Bruce Lipton was a stem-cell biologist whose groundbreaking work on cellular expression and epigenetics proved that *how* we think affects our physiology. Written plainly: the data you input into your body – physically, emotionally, and mentally – shapes who you become.

People often mistakenly believe that the DNA with which they were born is unchangeable; that their genetic code at birth is the only determinant of who they will become. Yet scientists have understood for decades that this genetic determinism is a flawed theory. At any given point in time, you have the opportunity to re-shape your reality. Your body is impacted at a cellular level by many external influences: weather, local pollution, what you eat, who you spend time with, the quality of your relationships and home life, how you internalize and manage the effects of stress, your ability to regulate and integrate intense emotions, how you move, and what stories you tell yourself about yourself.

So, if you think that you are somehow doomed because of who you are genetically, know that the opposite is true: your beliefs influence your biology. And the actions you take in accordance with those beliefs have a tangible influence on the outcome you set into motion. But no outcome is possible without that critical action step. Even if it seems to go wrong, or not the way you wished it would at first, trust that whenever you take a step toward your empowerment, desires, and highest ideals, your inner authority will rush to meet you.

Awareness and intention are the keys to self-mastery. Developing your relationship with all aspects of your embodied experience means that you have more information to work with and can make informed decisions based on listening to what exists. The body is the integration point, the place where we digest information and make decisions on future actions. With that in mind, approach your journey with the understanding that you are a multi-dimensional ecosystem that mirrors back what you put in. As you bring your awareness to the magic you already are, you will begin to appreciate the power of what is possible.

Reflection Questions:

1. What does a "no" feel like in your body? What does a "yes" feel like?

____

____

____

____

2. Recall an experience where you had a feeling about something and knew that it would all work out. Where in the body did your knowing register? What did it feel like to know?

____

____

____

____

3. Now recall a time where you felt something was off and things went badly. Where did you feel that? What were the sensations?

____

____

____

____

4. What relationship do you have with your body? What do you think about your body? What is the purpose of your body? How do you feel in your body? Do you love your body? How do you honor your body?

169

____

____

____

____

Actionable Practices:

1. Think about a big decision in your world – ideally something that you are not clear on yet.

    a. Hold that person, thing, or situation in your mind and do a gut check first: what are the subtle signals you are feeling there?

    ____

    ____

    ____

    ____

    b. What are you sensing about the people involved?

    ____

    ____

    ____

    ____

    c. Now do a fact check: Does the information make sense? Run the analysis, run the numbers, map it out, do background checks, etc. Do the details line up?

    ____

    ____

    ____

    ____

d. Do both the gut-check and the fact-check agree with one another? If not, what is your intuition trying to tell you? How can you follow-up?

____

____

____

____

2. What kind of self-care practice(s) would support you this week? Remember: it can be whatever makes you feel good! Taking a nice long run, playing a game with friends, cooking a beautiful meal, listening to sacred music, getting a massage, taking a bath. Identify three ways you could support yourself this week and then commit to doing them.

____

____

____

____

3. Try an energetic body practice that's new to you. This could be Yoga, Tai-Chi, Qi-Gong, Ecstatic dance, walking meditation, and so on.

4. Working with your Defining Moment again, journal the answers to these questions:

a. What was my body telling me?

____

____

____

____

b. Can I identify where, or what parts of my body,
   were sending strong signals?

____

____

____

____

c. Did I do a gut-check? Did I listen to it, or ignore it?

____

____

____

____

d. Can I discern today what my body was trying to tell
   me then? Does this change my experience/memo-
   ry and my understanding now?

____

____

____

____

Go Deeper:

1. *The Body Keeps the Score* by Bessel Van der Kolk

2. *Why We Sleep: Unlocking the Power of Sleep and Dreams* by Dr. Matthew Walker

3. *Yoga. Psyche. Soul.:* A Training with Ashley Turner

4. *Biology of Belief* by Bruce Lipton

CHAPTER 6

Wisdom
of the Heart

Mantra:

I give myself permission to connect deeply with my heart.

I give my heart permission to lead.

I give myself compassion and self-care.

I am connected to my source of truth and power.

I love myself.

Keywords:

Heart, Fire, Purification, Passion, Phoenix, Life Force,
Awakening, Embodiment

The heart is the true seat of power in the body. As you've moved through this book and engaged with the ideas here, you have been doing the work of establishing a new "anchor" in yourself, one less attached to the primacy of the mind as the dominant intelligence center. By now, you are ready to deepen your connection to your true seat of power and the voice of your inner authority: the heart. If you meditate on this, it will ring true: intuitively, the knowing within says "Yes!" I invite you now to step over this powerful threshold by saying "Yes" out loud in a bold way. Declare it like you are committing to a life-changing decision – because you are.

The heart center is where our inner authority evolves and arises. Our culture is long overdue for a reframe on the purpose of the heart. Not just a biological blood pump or the leading actor in teenage fairy tales, the heart is a primal source of the most potent transformational ingredient on the planet: love.

Many of us might feel conditioned to find the concept of love silly or naive. We might not have outwardly admitted it to ourselves because words like "heart" and "love" don't always feel safe to express, especially not in business. Yet whether you recognize it or not, your entire life is heart-centered. It's time to consciously bring this knowledge into the center of our decision making because the heart is where our inner authority lives.

The heart has already permeated every aspect of our lives and world. It's behind some of the largest social evolutionary movements of our time – like the call to center work around purpose, impact, and legacy; the "triple bottom line" of people, purpose, and profit; decentralized and people-powered economies like blockchain, crowdfunding, and crowdsourcing; work-life balance, sustainability metrics, and measures; environmentalism and the circular economy; increasing numbers of charities, nonprofits and foundations, social justice, inclusion, and equality initiatives; and the rise of conscious business leadership. The evidence is all around us and the common thread is a level of caring that didn't exist during the era of industrial capitalism.

The meteoric rise of the transformation economy is a powerful indicator of a new trend in business. As a culture and as people, we are working to transcend our materialism and connect with a deeper purpose. All around us are symptoms of a system reorganizing itself to better serve the people that exist within it. We see best-selling business books with titles about emotional intelligence, self-development, soft skills, the power of meditation to hone focus, and mindfulness in the workplace. Mysticism and spirituality are re-entering the mainstream conversation; no longer considered "fringe" as quantum physics and other modern sciences demonstrate the validity of ideas previously dismissed as "woo."

Yet what does all this have to do with the heart? For far too long, the heart has been left out of leadership. We celebrate and reward the "masculine" traits of leadership and authority – such as logical decision-making or aggressive strategy – yet you don't often see those same leaders taking the time to connect with their heart and integrate their feelings before doing so. This would most likely be considered a weakness in certain spaces.

Yet without this connection, we cannot integrate what we have experienced. In fact, we cannot truly evolve without our heart being online and operational. When we are integrated and aligned in ourselves, we communicate that integrity and authority through our actions. Our words are expressed and received differently when they come from the heart. Our heart is both vital and foundational to every aspect of our lives.

For many of you who operate in more masculinized professional environments, talking about love or the heart might feel uncomfortable at first. Rather than identify with any existing ideas about your heart and what it is or does, I instead invite you to contemplate what true coherence would look like for you. What would it feel like to be completely aligned with yourself? What would it feel like to have no confusion about who you are and what you are capable of? True coherence is a symptom of your heart doing exactly what it's supposed to do: unite all the systems of intelligence in your body so that they are in service to your evolution.

The Multi-Dimensional Nature of the Heart

The heart is the seat of sovereignty, soul, and your intuitive voice. It is your true home, where you can return to again and again in order to rest, to repair, to nourish, to cultivate, and to take action when the time is right. Everyone uses their heart to make decisions, whether they know it or not. Most of us use it more than we know, yet many hold the belief that to respond from your heart makes you weak when in fact, the heart is one of your deepest sources of power.

When I finally acknowledged my heart mattered and that I cared about what it had to say, my entire life changed. My results were better, my relationships were authentic, and I felt good inside because I was operating in alignment with my heart's desires. Yet, it wasn't enough for me to experience the results. I needed to understand what was happening.

I started to research the science of heart coherence and intelligence. I learned more about neurocardiology and how the heart circulates vital energy through the body. The more I explored, the more the big picture started to unlock. As I gained more insight into the body's inner workings and how they supported the overall system, I no longer wondered what had changed. Now, I knew how to actively engage the change and influence my future results. In other words, I started to hack the heart system so that I could better apply its teachings to my life. It was during this time that I began to formulate and experience my concept of inner authority. For the first time, I really understood what it meant to "come home" to myself.

The heart shows up in unexpected ways. In times of crisis, an incredibly challenging situation will create a tipping point that inevitably requires a group of people to come together and create solutions that don't exist. This wave of innovation starts internally, for in order to envision and implement new solutions, we actually need to do the work on ourselves *first*.

Brilliant ideas usually arrive when our old way of doing things is tested and fails. Being faced with a predicament that pushes us to go beyond our previous conceptions and assumptions challenges our brain to create new connections and evolve faster, forcing our consciousness to expand. A major tipping point that humanity encountered in 2020 was the pandemic. Followed by a massive global quarantine that effectively shut down the economy, the pandemic became the crucible for many people to go inwards and reflect on what needed to change. This unprecedented mass crisis forced millions of people to re-evaluate ways of living, playing, working, and loving almost overnight.

Even though the "normal" social fabric was no longer working, communities came together to show that social distancing and staying home wouldn't stop us from connecting and cultivating a new vision for our world. Countless stories started surfacing: people checking in on their neighbors, donating their stimulus checks to others in need, getting groceries for the elderly, or delivering lunches to the hundreds of thousands of school kids. Companies jumped in to provide aid and assistance before the American government. A new social network is emerging from the ashes of the old; one grounded in heart-centered action.

Among other things, the pandemic illuminated how the corporate focus on shareholders over stakeholders created an obscene wealth gap and staggering inequality in America; a gap few could have imagined when technology, science, and commerce were supposed to create prosperity, abundance, security, wealth, and health for all. Instead, the 99% watched as the 1% hoarded power, wealth, and resources in a heartless and soulless mission for total dominance. Yet, we know better and we can do better. The year 2020 became a tipping point because it made clear what we hadn't been able to fully look at: that things needed to change massively. The movements that emerged from this crisis demonstrate a crucial truth: that heart-centered, inclusive leadership is the way forward. The heart is our generation's

Rubicon: the boundary that defines where we are and who we are as humans.

The Heart Has a Brain

The heart is the true source of inner authority, which is why I prefer to think of the heart as our throne – the seat of sovereignty. If you are heart-led, then you make decisions from this center. In our heart, the most powerful and important emotions reside, for it is here that we can locate and generate love, compassion, and empathy. It is in the heart that our mental intelligence centers meet our emotional and instinctual intelligence centers: a place where we integrate many thoughts, feelings, and sensations into meaningful and coherent authentic expression.

Knowing when to use reason, logic, and analysis is important. However, if we rationalize our experiences without considering our emotions and instincts, we are only operating with half of the information necessary to make a truly authoritative decision. The left brain is quite powerful and can accomplish a lot, but we're only operating as half-humans if we're not including all of us.

The heart is so much more powerful than we realize. Often thought of as "secondary" to our cerebral intelligence centers, the heart is more than a simple blood pump. It has biological primacy, evidenced by the fact that it is the first organ to form during development in the embryo. Operating independently of your brain, the heart has its own neural network, interacts with the central nervous system, the autonomic nervous system, and the enteric nervous system. It also produces its own neuropeptides the molecules of emotion. We might think of our cerebral brain as the "mastermind" behind everything, but this idea is inaccurate, for the heart sends more information to the brain than the other way around. It is the *heart* that tells the *brain* what to do.

The heart brain is a highly complex information-processing center that communicates with and influences the cranial brain via the nervous system, hormonal systems, and other pathways. It is complex enough to sufficiently be considered a "brain *on* the heart," allowing it to act independently of the cranial brain to learn, remember, make decisions, and even feel and sense. If you've ever felt like your heart had a mind of its own, you would be exactly right!

The heart is incredibly magnetic, with a powerful field that can be detected up to three feet outside the body using special measuring tools. Enveloping every cell in your body and extending out in all directions around you, the heart has a bigger electromagnetic field than the brain or any other organ of the body and is 100 times greater in strength than the field generated by the brain. Whereas the brain is electric in energy polarity, projecting our thoughts and ideas out into the world, the heart is magnetic, attracting energy toward it.

You might notice that there are several neural networks in our incredible body. We've talked about the cerebral brain (Chapter 3), the emotional brain (Chapter 4), the gut brain (Chapter 5), and now, the heart brain. Each one is necessary for our bodies to be in total alignment. The human body is an interconnected system, and nothing works in a silo, so each of your intelligence centers influences and interacts with the rest. Understanding how and why these networks are integrated allows you to consciously access greater power, knowledge, and intuition over time.

Of course, the heart and mind work together, significantly impacting how we perceive and react to the world around us. You might have observed something interesting if you are someone who struggles to feel connected to their authentic decision making. Hesitation, doubt, insecurity, or overthinking delay and distract your heart's message from coming through. The mind has a tendency to distort the truth as it analyzes it. However, if you are listening deeply, you'll see that the heart's answer is immediate and immaculate. How interesting that we trust it less.

The Voice of the Heart

The biology of the heart is astounding the deeper you go into the details. Although many books could be written about the design of the heart alone, I wanted to provide a scientific baseline for us to build upon as we dive deeper into the ways we can unlock, open, and use our heart's innate strengths.

The heart is a power center where you can connect to, and access, the divine authority within. There is compelling scientific evidence to suggest that the heart does not operate within classical limits of time and space. This evidence comes from a rigorous experimental study that demonstrated the heart receives and processes data about future events before they actually happen. These studies seem to indicate that there is a central role our heart plays in processing and decoding truly intuitive information.

Beyond the parts that can be measured and quantified by science, there is the spiritual dimension that resides within our heart's center and is accessible through full faith and surrender. This space beyond form is so far past the linear models of the mind and intelligence in general that it requires a kind of faith to appreciate. This is the place of your embodiment.

When embodied in your heart, you become one with yourself – not a master *over* self, but a *Master of Self.* We've often heard the expressions "learn it by heart" and "speak from the heart" or "put your heart into it." Such expressions reflect this aspect of our spiritual intuitive heart. Throughout history, people have tuned into this space to find their inner voice, soul, or higher power – whatever one calls it, it is recognized as an unconditional and all-encompassing truth rooted in pure love. This is what great spiritual leaders and teachers of the times are revered for – not just the powerful wisdom they convey, but how they embody it entirely. This is what creates their powerful magnetism and helps them reach more people around the world.

Many traditions and wisdom lineages consider the heart to be the place where we communicate directly with our soul, higher self, big self, or inner divine authority. In that vein, there is a spiritual heart along with the physical heart organ and these communicate with each other both energetically as well as through the body's neural network and nervous system. When we begin to build a relationship with our heart, we start to understand that we have a unique, wise, and commanding voice that has real influence on our lives.

Closing Off the Heart Space

Now we have a deeper understanding of the biology of this powerful energy center. The heart is constantly attracting and receiving information and bringing it inwards. However, our heart can "shut down" and "turn off" too, effectively restricting the flow of information being processed by the body and the mind. This is often described as the heart feeling "closed" to the world or toward oneself. While it's not always a conscious decision, closing the heart *is* a form of protection. The heart usually closes when it doesn't feel safe or because it's been hurt and needs time to heal. Your heart is a delicate and finely tuned instrument that is highly capable of doing a lot – until it feels overwhelmed, rejected, or abandoned, and then it's easy to shut down.

This is normal and happens to most people many times in their lives. Feeling closed down in your heart space is common after a breakup or betrayal after you lose something important or feel injured or violated. Yet when our heart stays closed and doesn't open again, this severs us from an important source of information. It's alright to close your heart if you're scared but staying shut is a form of hurting yourself in the long run.

Closing your heart shuts down the opportunity to perceive the world fully. It dulls your ability to effectively utilize your senses and makes it more challenging to speak your truth clearly. Without the ability to fully access your intuitive nature, the big picture is harder to see. When you close your heart, you cut off the most essential intuitive sensing organ in your body, making it much harder to move toward what is meaningful and important for you. If you're struggling to see the connection to your business, start by considering your most important relationships in the workplace. How we communicate, connect, and collaborate with others is fueled by our ability to do the same with our hearts, for the two are intertwined. If you're not available to yourself, you're less likely to show up for anyone else.

Accomplishing important things requires collaboration with others – and that requires cultivating solid and trusting relationships with those that we live, work, love, and play with regularly. We can't approach business with just our brain and leave our heart at home, for connections require care and compassion; they require tending and understanding. Our heart is skilled at doing exactly this. The heart is known to produce a powerful social bonding hormone known as oxytocin, which acts as a neurotransmitter and has been shown to increase tolerance, trust, friendship and the establishment of pair-bonds.

There are many mechanisms and situations that shut our heart down along with our connection to it. Fear, trauma, personal narratives, and projections are several common ways in which the heart is silenced and shut. Many of us struggle with the need to be right, to control others' actions, to condemn or judge when we don't understand something, or feel uncomfortable. If you want to show up as a leader, then it's essential that you work on strengthening your heart's resilience, so you can bear witness to what wants to be seen and shared, rather than shutting down in the face of conflict or confusion.

The heart has a natural expansion and contraction. The more you pay attention to your heart and center yourself in different emotions, the more you'll start to become aware of the difference between an open, receptive heart and a closed, rigid one. When the events of 2020 hit – the pandemic, the economic crisis, the crisis of leadership, and the social justice uprisings, we witnessed many people shut down their hearts as they confronted the intensity and shock of the situation. Fear was pervasive, and it was challenging for many people to navigate the unknown from a place of love as they lost jobs, family members, and a sense of normalcy.

When the pandemic first hit, I watched myself go into survival mode too: my mind was constantly in tactical mode, scanning approaching situations for danger and making appropriate preparations. I noticed that I was spending a lot of time reflecting on potential downside scenarios that might occur: What if we went into military lockdown? What if people started looting or rioting in my neighborhood? What if the global financial system collapsed? *What if people didn't care about one another anymore?*

I noticed that in many instances I felt panic. I remembered my tools and re-centered myself in my heart space. I calmed down and slowed down. I was feeling fear not just for myself but for everyone around me – yet it wasn't helping. So, I started to "think" and respond from my heart. I started reflecting on how I could support others I was connected with in meaningful ways. Even though I didn't feel totally financially secure, I wanted to support my community and start from a different place. I began reaching out to small businesses that I interacted with regularly– like my doggy daycare and local cleaning services and restaurants – to see how I could support them in this time. I gave the grocery delivery people bigger tips since it mattered more now. These actions didn't save the world, but they did make a difference.

In doing this, I noticed that I naturally started to shift out of fear and into a genuine state of gratitude. I experienced myself feeling more connected to others around me. I took my Circle of Sovereignty online and made it a point to share more stories on social media of companies, celebrities, executives, and others who were stepping up and demonstrating heart-led leadership as the various crises unfolded. I decided to emphasize the good that was present, and it shifted my entire focus. Helping others became the lifeline to helping myself.

The Fear Filter

The heart is often associated with courage. The word courage comes from "coeur," the French word for *heart*. We must connect with our source of courage in order to overcome fears, shame, and shoulds when we are faced with the terrifying, the unexpected, or the insurmountable. That's the job of the heart, from which we draw our resolve and inner strength.

Fear blocks intuition. It also jams rational decision-making and impedes key physical and emotional expansion. Fear is both simple and complex in how it functions in our body. On the one hand, it's very easy to understand how fear is directly connected to our survival functions: the body goes into "Fight, Flight, or Freeze" mode and, as we've learned in previous chapters, shuts down its non-vital functions under duress, stress, or survival. Fear is a real feeling – with profound physical effects that alert us to its presence. Whether it's a jolt of energy in a dangerous situation, a tingling in your stomach, goosebumps, or a voice that says "Nope," fear is an indicator of something feeling off in our field.

Yet fear is also nuanced because our environment, lifestyle, society, and programming have instilled fear into the very fabric of our existence. Most of us experience some aspect of our internal programming when we encounter something that feels uncomfortable to our sense of security and safety. We fear losing our jobs or having that difficult conversation with a colleague; we worry about someone's reaction to our truth and fear that they might judge us. While these concerns carry their own intense emotions and energetic charge, they aren't true fears in the real, physical, sense of the word. Our bodies may feel discomfort, and the emotions of anxiety may come up due to worrisome thoughts, but is this actually fear?

It's important to reframe the role of fear. When we develop a neurosis, we become agitated by our fearful thoughts and obsessive thinking rather than deal with the actual thing we're afraid of. Many of us are overwhelmed with stresses that affect our thoughts, emotions, and physiology every day, without much time to relax and release all the stresses impacting our systems. Constant stress and burnout deeply impact your overall wellness levels: your body interprets stress as a constant, low-level danger, which makes it hard for your systems to function normally over extended periods of time.

Since thoughts of "fear" trigger parasympathetic physiological responses, a powerful centering practice is to ask yourself: "Am I truly afraid, or do I *think* I'm afraid?" Tune into your body, breathe into your chest, and ask your heart for guidance.

Fear is the polar opposite of love. It is the primal feeling from which all negative emotions and responses arise. From anxiety to rage, these lower vibrational feelings can be hard to deal with. We tend to lash out when we're in a fearful place. Abandonment, separation, rejection, and humiliation are all states that we want to avoid at all costs. On a deeper level, we fear these feelings because many of us are protecting ourselves from feeling them again. We already know how deeply they hurt, and we do not desire to experience those emotions again.

The good news is that we cannot sustain fear and love at the same time. When we feel into the fear, we realize it's not our natural state. It doesn't feel good and we don't like to stay there. The heart is where we deal with and overcome the fears we carry; the place where we generate our most powerful and empowering emotions, and feeling what life brings us. You might be relieved to realize that fear cannot come from the heart nor can it exist there for any length of time. This is why we go to our heart to locate our courage, our bravery, our compassion, and our gratitude. Consider your heart as your Sanctuary of Sovereignty from here on out, for fear cannot live there.

If you want to know if something is true, filter it through your heart before making a decision or coming to a conclusion. The more you do this, the more you'll notice false truths and ideas dropping away. Fear hides the truth because it wants to protect itself. This is how fear survives: by not being confronted by the brave heart. The heart is our true self, our true power, the voice of our inner authority; the divine one who trusts completely and without reservation. If you are still wondering why it's important to have a relationship with your heart, the simple reason is this: you'll become fearless. Real power is the ability to connect to your heart's truth and bring forward the desires, hopes, dreams, and intentions that live there, waiting to be discovered by you.

The Inner Conflict

The most challenging conflict you'll face in your lifetime is the one between your heart and your ego. The easiest way to think about your ego is as your programming personified. It's the part of you that believes that things should be or go a certain way to get what you want (control), stay emotionally protected (safety), and socially accepted (survival). But the ego is not you! The unchecked ego is dangerous because it believes that in order to satisfy the ideas you have about yourself and life, you should do things in a specific way – one that feels out of alignment with your authentic self. For example: maybe you are unhappy at work and you want to start your own business, but instead, you stay because you think this is what success looks like or what your family expects. If you are acting out of internal alignment with yourself in order to satisfy some false condition – acting aggressively with a client when you know a different approach would be more authentic – then you are in your ego.

When was the last time you felt conflicted? What recent situation made you question your decision or challenge your typical way of doing things? Did you experience your mind telling you to do it a certain way even though that particular approach felt wrong or off? If you're familiar with this situation, then it's important to slow down and notice what comes up when you get close to your confusion. Where does the root of the conflict live? As you investigate your internal landscape, you might find that an emotion exists there – perhaps a voice that says "No, this isn't the right path." If something feels off in our heart, it usually is, even if you can't explain it.

When we're not tuned into our heart space, it easily leads to unconscious violence and abuse in our emotions, words, and actions. If we are not connected to the choice in our heart, it holds the power to hurt others easily, for it is not conscious nor centered in loving action. We see this playing out in the world on a larger scale: unjust and inhumane policies emerge from abuses of power; from a lack of caring and compassion for the people who will be impacted by such regulations and rules that often benefit a specific group. Ego often plays out as identification, manifests as behavior, and creates all sorts of energetic and physical results that might look impressive on the surface but don't feel good deep down inside.

The ego operates from fear, protectionism, lack, and scarcity. Its role is to create an acceptable identity that compares, contrasts, and competes with others. Consider it the collective sum of all your programming, fears, worries, doubts, insecurities, and self-aggrandizing or self-deprecating behaviors. When operational, it keeps us disconnected from our true source of power: the throne of our heart. When we ignore a problem rather than face it head-on, we make it worse. This reveals that the internal conflict we're experiencing is actually being projected onto our external surroundings in order for us to see it clearly. Emotional energy such as anger is powerful but unconsciously projecting it on others causes more harm than it clears. The conflict between our ego and heart can feel like very dissonant energy that doesn't feel good and only creates further chaos and confusion.

Dissonance and Resonance

Connection is the way of the heart. Thanks to technology and global commerce, we're more connected to each other in many invisible ways. While this has caused a lot of overwhelm and disinformation, it also has opened up a lot of opportunities for deeper connectivity. Your internal state of coherence matters and impacts others that you're in relation with. Whether personally or professionally, the ripple effects of our energies extend out into the world. If we're in a state of alignment, we'll see aligned results come forward. If we're in a state of internal dissonance, we'll experience that instead. That's why it's so important to tend to our internal states and get curious about what's happening.

Let's put it this way: have you ever been in an argument? Have you been able to catch yourself *before* starting the argument and thought about how to handle it in a different way? What happened when you went in guns blazing? What happened when you came from a more centered place?

It's hard to do precise, focused work when you're thinking about an argument you had that morning. Or perhaps you've noticed that it's harder to cook a delicious meal when you're sad. It's hard to get into things that we're not truly feeling, and when we force ourselves to keep going anyway, we often make things worse for ourselves. When I'm angry or frustrated, I can't think straight and can't do much except physical things like working out or chores. I enjoy doing detail-oriented tasks like balancing my household budget when I'm calm and even-keeled. I cook my favorite meals when I'm enthusiastic. While I consider myself to be a good friend who listens well, if I'm depleted, I'm not good at holding space for anyone, including myself. When I'm in a coherent state, I'm effective in any and every situation.

The heart is a vital sensing organ. The moments where you feel completely in tune with yourself, when life feels like it's magically unfolding for you in perfect timing, are representative of the state of resonance. We've all had experiences of resonance with other people, ideas, and situations, whether we consciously know it or not. While this might sound like a woo way to put it, resonance in physics describes the same phenomenon that I'm describing. When waves of light, sound, or energy move, they vibrate. If several waves of sound (such as in a song, for instance) vibrate at the same rate, they make a rhythmic wave that is harmonic and flows naturally.

However, when several different waves travel at different frequencies it creates erratic patterns: this is dissonance. It creates a disharmonious, jagged pattern where each wave is doing something different, resulting in a feeling of discombobulation and confusion – just as we experience in our hearts when things aren't aligned or congruent in our intelligence centers. Coherence, then, is a deep resonance with all aspects of our being. When the mind, heart, and nervous system are operating on the same wavelength, we feel the effects of that deep in our system. We easily flow with our inner authority and our intuition.

Research has proven that coherence in the body can be measured by electromagnetic signals between the heart, lungs, and brain using Heart Rate Variability (HRV), a way of measuring the time interval between heartbeats. Erratic variations in heart rate produce erratic thoughts, expressions, and behaviors, which in turn leads to physiological exhaustion and chronic disease. If you've ever felt anxious, nervous, or panicked, you'll most likely remember the go-to solution: three deep breaths. It turns out there's a reason for that – when you establish coherence in breath, it resonates with your heartbeat, which establishes a coherence in your mind because they are all linked.

Coherence is the ultimate "end game" of meditation and other mindfulness modalities, as it establishes alignment throughout all the intelligence centers of the body, making it easier for them to function at their highest levels of harmony. There are numerous proven benefits of creating more coherence in your system: your cortical functions are enhanced, enabling greater objectivity and intuitive perception; your internal systems work seamlessly together to exchange information; and finally, your focus, performance, and attention spans are shown to increase. When you are heart-centered and coherent, you are better able to navigate your thoughts and emotions over time, creating a deeper connection with your inner voice. When you operate from your heart-center you bring all your intelligent centers into coherence; resulting in harmonious, effective, and efficient decision-making and action-taking. In other words: *this* is the definition of productive intuition in action.

Heart-Based Leadership Through Coherence

Operating from the heart goes beyond personal empowerment. Many people don't feel safe bringing their heart out in the workplace or in professional environments where they don't feel welcome to show up as their whole selves. Rather than try and find ways to express more authentically, they disconnect entirely. If we're afraid to speak up and express what's on our hearts, we're ineffective, inefficient, unmotivated, and largely unproductive. We're certainly not going to be enthusiastic or creative.

The culture around leadership and success has traditionally been rigid, emphasizing an aggressive approach that proves one "right" and often rewards force and winning (at all costs) over compassion, empathy, and collaboration. Those who didn't adhere to the traditional way of doing things were overlooked as leaders or excluded from critical decision-making conversations. But, there has been a shift. Intuition is increasingly cited as a leadership competence and companies are willing to talk about intuitive heart decisions. Founders, executives, and leaders are asking, "How do we harness intuition as a practical tool for business?"

Stress is a business issue, and more companies are recognizing the need to address their employees' wellbeing with coaching, mentorship, mindfulness practices, and centering techniques such as heart coherence.

Organizations that have worked with evidence-based heart-coherence tools and techniques, like those offered by the HeartMath Institute, have reported measurable, sustained, improvements in both work-related and personal metrics. For example, one company reported that six months after their initial training they were seeing over 50% improvement in productivity, teamwork, and empowered action. In another company, 70% of staff were still experiencing ongoing benefits such as positive behavioral changes, lower stress levels, and improved overall health and wellbeing. These are two of many organizational case studies proving that the heart has a place – in addition to playing an important role – in business.

With heart-based coherence, people are able to better manage stress responses (emotional, psychological, and physical) in the moment, improve mental clarity and decision-making, increase focus, and listen better. Individuals build resilience, respond to change and challenges in new ways, and have described feeling more present, flexible, and in flow. Organizations have reported ROI and measurable benefits such as improvements in communication, the ability to create collaborative team environments, engage innovation, sustain employee engagement, retain staff, and achieve positive cultural shifts.

Heart-coherence techniques and training from organizations such as The HeartMath Institute and The Institute for Applied Meditation on the Heart have become a mainstay of my personal and professional practice. When we shift our state into coherence by recalling genuine feelings of appreciation or caring, we access the heart's intelligence. When we can access the heart's intelligence, we can directly ask and immediately receive answers to our most pressing questions. Whether it's decision making, problem solving, or creative ideation, the heart readily provides intuitive insights. If you are wondering how to harness your intuition, the answer is: by asking the heart.

The heart's intelligence, heart coherence, and your intuition are all linked. Intuition provides direct *perception* and the heart provides direct *connection* to greater aspects of transcendent intelligence. By building coherence, the head and the heart work together, allowing us to open up to expanded dimensions of information and insights that make a positive impact on our roles, relationships, and organizations. We need more heart-centered leaders who don't sweat the small stuff and dare to operate from their heart's intuitive intelligence.

The Heart Path to Total Embodiment

The heart defines the nature of what we allow into our lives. When we are in coherence, we experience clarity and alignment with our inner authority. The more we radiate a clear, open, and truthful heart, the more powerful our force of attraction becomes, thus naturally drawing in that which fulfills the heart's passion.

When you can acknowledge, accept, and embrace the heart as a place of deep intuitive intelligence and insight, your life will change permanently. You will find the truth and recognition that you were seeking outside yourself and realize that it's always been inside and is now easier to access. Perhaps all your mind needed was a way to validate the heart's truth using the tools it accepted: science, facts, data.

Hopefully, now you have begun to recognize your heart as an intelligent, multifaceted instrument of attunement and alignment. Now that your logical, analytical mind has a "reason" to accept the incredibly important role of the heart in your life, you can begin the process of embodiment: of being allied with your inner authority.

My goal in this book is to help you accept and embrace your whole self with utter trust and total love. Having been through my journey of awakening, reckoning, and acceptance, I can share with full courage and confidence that the heart knows what's best for you, and will communicate what you need to know when you ask.

What does it mean to become aware of your inner authority? What does it mean to align with your intuitive nature? It means knowing where your true power lives – in your heart. The science behind these ideas is measurable. This isn't about "positive vibes only" – there is proven data backing up all the concepts shared here. What these evidence-based theories and approaches prove to me is something critically important to your success: if there's no force and no organ in the human body more powerful than the heart, then the power of love is proven to be profound. It's time to tap that reservoir for your own wellbeing. If you don't love yourself, then you haven't tapped into your full power source. If you harbor bad thoughts towards yourself (many of us do) then you're consistently training your body to hold the negativity, register it as normal, and drain your energy.

To fully tap into the transformational power of the heart we can use three powerful energetic allies: forgiveness, compassion, and gratitude. These fundamental, daily practices help us become better tenders of our heart and thus, of others. Forgiving yourself makes it easier to forgive others. Compassion for yourself makes it easier to extend it to others. Gratitude for who you are *and* for those around you make your life meaningful.

Loving yourself is paramount to changing your entire life outcome. It sounds too easy (or too difficult, perhaps) to be true, but self-love is the most important ingredient in your personal alchemy. It might not feel like something you believe just yet, but don't overthink that. Focus on connecting to your heart and sending love to your body like you would smile at a baby. It can be that gentle, that simple, to start. The reality is that no one is going to love us enough if we can't learn to love ourselves. Otherwise, what happens is we find ourselves chasing love around, hoping that it will finally turn around and face us; find us worthy. But love is self-fulfilling: the more you give to yourself, the more you get.

Remember: your heart is magnetic, so the more you strengthen it with love, the more it attracts miraculous things into your world. You are the one holding the key that unlocks the love and lets it flow, so why not start now? Find time today to look yourself in the eyes and love on yourself. Find time every day to reflect on the love you have for your life, your family, your work, your home, your world. Even if it feels challenging, the truth is that you can love it as is – and that's where the real work lives. Give yourself over to love today and try it out.

Like attracts like. The more you love yourself, the more your energy shifts into higher frequencies, creating ripple effects of intention. Your heart sends the energy of love out into the world and it comes back to you like magic – only it's magnetics. That's why the more you love yourself the more love will come back to you amplified. You receive the energy you put out into the world. Take a minute and reflect: what have you been putting out into the world lately? Are you projecting fear, anger, disappointment, hopelessness? Or are you shining trust, hope, peace, joy, abundance, and love?

This is not to say that trusting love is always the easier path – in fact, for many, it's very hard to love ourselves properly. If you find yourself triggered or uncovering stigma around the idea of love, notice and observe what emotions come up. What narrative exists for you? Do you think love is good, bad, or something else entirely? What labels or expectations have you put on the idea of love?

At the end of the day, love is our life force. Love is what creates life, and thus the world around us. If you find yourself thinking that love is bad, then perhaps it's time to examine why those beliefs exist and who put them there in the first place. Because I know you weren't born with them. Some of you might have grown up around the idea that to express love for yourself was synonymous with selfishness or arrogance. Here's the thing: love is not vanity. Love is not narcissistic in its purest form. Love encompasses many different expressions and realities, but all are rooted in the uncondi-tional embrace of what is already perfect. In this way, love is acceptance and self-respect. It is recognition of yourself as someone that matters, even if no one is more special than another. Love is honoring yourself so that you know how to take good care of yourself and take pride in doing so. Love polishes the soul and gives us radiance as we learn to relax into its glow. When you trust yourself, it's easy to trust others and extend them the same grace. This is the gift that love gives us.

Embrace Your Self

The programming most of us we grew up with taught us that loving ourselves is selfish, and that's where the seed of disempowerment starts. We grow up inside a culture that makes money off our self-loathing, for we've been taught that our bodies, faces, and features are only lovable if they fit the stereotypical ideas of beauty and strength peddled in the media.

Yet the love you hold in your heart space is a force that can be harnessed regardless of what you look like and regardless of whether someone else decided you fit a standard. Love is a superpower, and it's available to everyone – that's why choosing love is always the radical choice and has been for most of history. We might think love is more fitting to the bedroom than the boardroom, but if you see a difference then you're missing the whole point. Love is what enables life. We begin there.

Start by giving yourself permission to love yourself. Declare it to yourself, to the mirror, to a friend, to the world. Try and trust that statement and see what hap-pens. Let it be your mantra for the next hour or day or week. You are now dismantling the idea that loving yourself is shameful, selfish, or bad. You are actively re-writing the story that to love yourself takes love away from someone else. As you affirm that you love yourself each day, you'll start to reprogram your heart and mind to feel and be more coherent.

If you begin each day with self-love as your baseline, you will soon find that you have become a force to be reckoned with because you are no longer vying for validation, affirmation, and attention to prove your worth. Your worthiness is no longer conditional. You'll find yourself expressing your love, truth, and power in ways that feel good, and you'll start to see life flow more easily as you take action from your heart center. Love is the difference between assertiveness and aggression.

The more you listen to your heart, the more you'll find that your truth is revealing itself to you in every moment. It will become noticeably clearer and louder as you continue the truth in your heart. The way you show up will shift and your presence will feel different. You'll quickly see who's willing to meet you there, in the heart, and who isn't ready. You will align yourself more easily and naturally with coherence and resonance, rather than dissonance.

How you express and receive love might be different from other people in your world, so take the time to find the flavor of love that tastes the best to you. Get to know what you need. Are you someone who needs a lot of acknowledgment? Or do you feel best when people give you space? Knowing your "ingredients" makes it easier to communicate clearly and confidently what you need. If you haven't already, it's time to start cultivating your relationship with your heart. Learning how to love yourself through the good and bad, the anticipated and the unexpected, is how you build the resilient, courageous, and compassionate heart at the center of a satisfying and successful life.

Reflection Questions:

1. Where is there resonance in your body? Where is there resistance? Can you notice the difference without judging it or defining it? Try expressing it like you would describe a painting to a blind person.

____

____

____

____

2. Think about a time, situation, or moment when you "knew" something important and you felt it in your heart. How did you know you knew? What did that feel like for you?

____

____

____

____

3. In what ways, and in what situations, do you shut
    down or close off your heart? What happens next?
    Reflect on the consequences, responses, and out-
    comes of operating from a closed heart. Ask yourself
    why you shut down? Then, ask yourself how you can
    trust your heart to stay open.

____

____

____

____

Actionable Practices:

1. Ask Your Heart: When you have a question that you can't resolve with the usual mental analyses, something is weighing on you, or you simply wish to receive deeper guidance on an issue, try the simple technique of asking your heart.

   a. Get a notebook, journal, or piece of paper. Sit quietly in meditation, deepen your breathing, and start to place your focus on your heart area.

   b. Send a few breaths to your heart space, and imagine that it is expanding and supporting you.

   c. When you are ready, silently ask your heart for guidance or an answer to your query.

   d. Sit quietly and notice the answer. It can come in many different forms.

   e. Write down the answers that you receive.

   f. When you are complete, close your eyes again, breathe a few more times into your heart space, and express your gratitude for its wisdom, guidance, and support.

2. Take time to actively feel and express your gratitude every day for a week. This could look like setting aside five minutes at the end of each day to list the things you are grateful for, or this could be implementing a practice of expressing gratitude when you come up against frustration.

____

____

____

____

3. Working with your Defining Moment again, journal the answers to these questions:

a. What was my heart telling me? What subtle messages was it sending?

____

____

____

____

b. Did I shut down my heart? If so, why?

____

____

____

____

c. Was there something you wished you could express, but didn't?

____

____

____

____

d. What do I understand now, from the heart's perspective, that I didn't understand then?

____

____

____

____

Go Deeper:

1. *Science of the Heart: Exploring the Role of the Human Heart* by Rollin McCraty

2. Hridaya Yoga: www.hridaya-yoga.com

3. I Am Heart: www.iamheart.org

CHAPTER 7

Wisdom of the Spirit

Mantra:

I am intuitive. I am powerful.

I trust my inner authority. I am sovereign.

I give my intuitive wisdom permission to guide me.

I open to my transcendent intelligence.

Keywords:

Spirit, Ether, Space, Source,

Timelessness, Knowingness, Surrender, Void

True intuition *is* transcendent. Throughout this book, we have been exploring the many forms of intelligence that exist within you. As you can see, there are many brains, many centers, and many ways your intuition communicates. Enclosing all of that is your divine intelligence center – the original source of knowledge. Transcendent intelligence is your spiritual brain – the subtle knowing that feels channeled from the infinite. Your direct connection to Source, Soul, and the Self is here, and it comes through as authentic wisdom.

The "knower" within is the ultimate authority. This center is intangible and invisible, yet inherently present, deeply felt, and undeniable. Whether or not you recognize it, your entire life experience is designed to help you embody this state of being.

There is no "there" to get to – so let's begin where you are. The transcendent intelligence that we will explore next is not out there, nor is it a future destination. It's right here, right now. Where you are, as you are. Remember: your experience of the transcendent intelligence living within you may be different than someone else's.

Over the course of this book, you have been undergoing an internal evolution. If you have integrated and engaged with the teachings, you will already have received many opportunities to put this knowledge and wisdom into practice.

In this chapter, we cross an important threshold. I've shared the most relevant scientific research and personal stories that have shaped my evolution in order to give you a foundation for the deeper work ahead. As we move forward, know that you are being invited to unearth, unlock, and embody your divine inner authority.

Go Beyond Knowing

An exciting interweaving of science and spirituality is underway at this very moment. Humans are more invested than ever before in self-discovery, and understanding the applications of consciousness tools with greater awareness and enthusiasm. More and more, people are tuning into an expanding body of research that proves the scientific validity of ideas previously dismissed as esoteric, mystical, occult, or fantastical. Now, quantum physics, neurobiology, immunology, and psychology are demonstrating that we can transform and manipulate many, if not all, aspects of our life through enhanced awareness and practice.

The foundations of life are built on a double helix. The structure of DNA seems to indicate that what at first appears separate is actually intricately connected. Science and spirituality used to exist in vastly different worlds that didn't communicate. Now, we are beginning to see proof that they support each other.

This integration is also mirrored in ourselves. Your experience is the axis on which your truth turns, and so part of the work you are being asked to do is trust your intuition – your inner authority – rather than reach for an authority outside of yourself.

What's the difference between body wisdom, mind wisdom, emotional wisdom, heart wisdom, and spiritual wisdom? They are all aspects of one, unified wisdom – transcendent, immanent, and available through intuitive guidance. One of my biggest lessons as I started to awaken was realizing that I hadn't trusted my intuition for a very long time. I had been so fixated on finding success, validation, and authority in structures outside of myself that I wasn't trusting the transcendent intelligence within. That woke me up. Not only was I suppressing my experience and emotions, but I was suppressing my connection with the source of everything: the luminous matrix of life itself.

Intuition is the process of perceiving or knowing something without conscious reasoning. Some researchers believe that intuition is an innate ability and potentially one of the most natural we possess. The ability to intuit could be regarded as an inherited, yet unlearned gift. We already have it; we just need to learn how to locate and activate its powers.

Intuition is more than a gift – it's a fundamental function of being human. Like every other aspect of our body, it contributes immense value to the whole. It is a sense, it is like a muscle or an ability that can be strengthened, developed, and honed over time.

When we talk about the ultimate Source; Universe, God, Tao, or Great Spirit, it can be helpful to think of it as the field of electromagnetic frequencies that every being exists within and is intricately connected to. Everything emerges from and engages with this Field. Connecting with the Field bypasses the cumbersome processes of the physical human brain and goes straight to the source of universal self-organizing intelligence. This is what intuition connects us with on the most essential level. It's direct knowing, without any extra work, thinking, analyzing, or research.

Intuition is the Wise One within. The most helpful definition of wisdom that I've found is a quality of knowledge and experience that contains loving discernment. Wisdom is a form of perception that penetrates to the true essence of a matter or an idea. It is built on accumulated learning and experience, and it often emerges as an immediate and instant knowing.

It's never too late to reconnect. Even if you feel disconnected from yourself and your inner authority, the first step is to get into a coherent state. For some, this might be meditation or Qi Gong, for others, it might be dancing. Whatever you choose, the point is to disengage from the mental chatter and emotional drama of the moment and come back to yourself. Meditation is a disciplined practice for this reason: the better we can become at tuning out the noise and tuning into the Self, the more we can clear out the energies and ideas that don't serve.

Bringing an awareness practice into your life will have profound effects on your ability to create a life you love and manifest from a place of inner authority. It will bring a different level of peace and fulfillment than any external attainment or distraction. All you have to do is start listening to what wants to emerge from within.

Yes, You Are Probably Psychic

As you dive deeper into your innate intuitive powers and wisdom, you will inevitably start to realize that the answers you seek are available immediately if you know how to listen. This might feel "magical" or "otherworldly." but the reality is much simpler than that: your body's natural abilities are operating at full capacity!

When I was going through my awakening, I was interested in finding answers. My journey took me into many different directions. Although I originally held a lot of stigma about the esoteric and mystical teachings I was encountering in my research, the more I investigated the more I saw that science and spiritual philosophies affirmed the same basic theories. This led me to question where my conditioning existed, and whether I was giving myself the opportunity to understand what was happening. I didn't want to be seen as a weirdo, yet I *was* intrigued by what I found. It resonated with me, so I pushed past the egoic-mental resistance and plunged in.

As I deepened my studies and started applying more of the practices that I was finding in both the scientific and spiritual realms, I started to notice a palpable shift: I was becoming more psychic. Said another way: I was accessing and putting to use my intuition, which was cultivating a deeper trust in my ability to take action with authority. Working with all my intelligence centers created more coherence at a foundational level. This gave me access to my inner knowing, which is what many people are describing when they mention psychic abilities.

Activating your psychic nature does not require that you take a blood oath or swear allegiance to the devil. Psychics don't know what the future will look like, nor can they predict it. Rather, they are consciously accessing a wealth of information in the Field, on command, or that is being presented to them. The coherence in their field allows them to clarify and translate this information more rapidly and accurately than most people who remain undeveloped in their abilities. Another thing: they trust both the information they receive, and their ability to receive it. They stay open, non-judgmental, and objective. This is called holding space or being a clear channel or vessel. You take your self (ego, mind, thoughts, personality, etc.) out of the picture so to speak, and you allow wisdom, intuition, and transcendent intelligence to come *through* and *into* you.

If this idea excites you, great! There's nothing to be afraid of. The more I allowed myself to engage with these intelligence centers more consciously, the more thrilling and satisfying life became, for I was able to respond from a place of empowered action. I wrote this book because I was excited to share my findings with others like me – people who value both scientific and spiritual inquiry, who find value in the esoteric as well as the rational, and who are committed to becoming their most authentic and empowered self through trust and discernment.

It might feel easier when you're stuck to ask someone else for an answer. Yet in going outside of ourselves, we give our power away to others – whether its other people, systems, institutions, or collective beliefs. Understanding and accessing your intuition is the empowered path, yet it can often take a while to trust yourself and know what feels aligned and true for you.

Developing the ability to work with *all* the layers of your intuition will take you farther in the long run. If your definition of success is based on what others think, then you will struggle to feel sovereign in your life. Your success and happiness are ultimately your responsibility to cultivate, whether or not people agree with every single one of your choices. When you are connected to your intuition, other people's opinions matter less, for you are clear on what you need. You do what's right for you.

This is what it means to take your power back. We give our power away when we expect others to solve our problems, give us direction, manage our emotions, or soothe our insecurities. When you commit to coming from your inner authority, rooted in your intuitive nature, you take control of yourself. You decide who you are and what will be, for you already have the answers within.

The insight others give us can be helpful, but in the end, we need to integrate and implement our own solutions. That's why opinions belong to others; they have the right to express them but you don't have the obligation to follow them, especially if their opinion is highly charged, constricting, shoulding, or demeaning. For example, an insensitive remark or comment on your social media channel doesn't need to stay there. That person can say whatever they want but you certainly don't have to give them a platform – especially your own – to do so. On a different tack, when you go to a doctor about a health problem more than likely they tell you what they see, provide an opinion, and offer a solution. In the end, it is still up to you to schedule the follow-up recommendations, whether that's surgery, taking your vitamins, and doing the work of healing yourself. You have support and expertise to point the way forward, but in the end, the real effort is on you. Take other people's opinions with a grain of salt and pass them through your filter of truth. Does this feedback work for you? Does it come from a place of non-attachment? Does this person have the ability to truly be honest with you? We have *all* given opinions with our motives, conscious or unconscious, beneath our well-intentioned "advice." Therefore, discernment, like focus, is a foundational tool to self-mastery.

There are many ancillary tools that assist our inner work, and these will depend, as always, on what is intuitively right for you. Tools look very different depending on what you are working on and what dimension you are working within. A tool like a therapist can be very helpful in navigating chaotic or confusing emotional terrain. A doctor is a powerful tool if you are addressing an issue in the body. In the same way, there are many tools that can be supportive when one ventures deeper into the subtle layers of the transcendent intelligence centers. Astrology, numerology, tarot cards, runes, dream interpretation, and divination are all tools that help us to interpret and translate the symbols, myths, and archetypes that dwell in our deeper unconscious and spiritual layers. I resonate with astrology and use it as an energetic evolutionary tool to unearth and accept the many seemingly conflicting aspects of my personality and to understand my soul's path. Most of these tools help clarify hidden behavioral patterns and archetypal symbols that are operational, if invisible, to us. When you look beneath the watered-down, pop-culture use of these often discredited, ancient, and powerful tools, you'll find that they hold answers that speak directly to your intuition; to the mind beyond the mind.

There are many ways we can unlock and engage our natural intuitive psychic abilities. You don't need to be a mystic or shaman, a "lightworker" or healer, to work with this innate gift. It is there, and you decide when you are ready to use it.

Whether you are ready to believe it or not, with enough practice you can sense and develop your "divine eye" which is what *clairvoyance* means: seeing beyond the everyday and simultaneously into the deeper depths and farthest reaches of your being. The "clair" refers to the non-local, inner senses that can be perceived when you start tapping into this transcendent center: clairvoyance (deep seeing), clairaudience (deep listening), clairsentience (deep feeling), and claircognizance (deep knowing). Considered by many to be the "technologies of the sacred" these abilities are not reserved for the enlightened gurus and spiritual teachers. To quote the visionary Henry Ford: "Whether you believe you can, or you can't, you're right." What would you rather believe about yourself?

The Wise Realm of the Mystics

I've never been one to take things at face value. I'm not a contrarian on purpose, I just need to know myself what is right for me. I've learned through a lot of trial and error. Even though I've built a career in the grounded world of finance and investing, I've always sought out transformation and self-mastery. This may be the reason I wrote my thesis on the role of emotional intelligence in intercultural management, or why I started listening to neuro-linguistic programming (NLP) audiobooks and using binaural meditation tools in my early twenties. As a seeker of knowledge, I don't rest at simple surface explanations – I dive into the deep and research everything: the established facts, the progressive theories, and yes, the esoteric teachings. I don't accept anyone else's programming as the conditions that I live within. I have to experience everything for myself; it's the only way I can learn what is right and true for me.

If I am honest, the word "spiritual" triggers me. It's been co-opted and distorted. Like most profound truths and teachings, there are many versions of spirituality, and not all of them are empowering to the holders of the beliefs. It takes a lot to disentangle ourselves from the ideology and extract the core truths without confusing them. We can't avoid bias, for it exists, even in the most rigorous scientific research paper. Instead, you must learn to be discerning.

I'm not here to tell anyone what spirituality means, for that is a very personal journey, unique to every person who undertakes it. If I am here to teach anything, it is to listen to your intuition and trust yourself. Redefine words and concepts so that they align with your inner authority. Ask yourself: What does spirituality mean to you? Then trust yourself enough to listen deeply.

During the first three years of my awakening, I felt a lot of discomfort. I was triggered, resisting, exploring, accepting, removing, and redefining what the word spiritual meant because none of the definitions I had found worked for me. They didn't fully encapsulate what I was experiencing in my own awakening. Many self-certified "experts" were more than happy to tell me what to do or how to be spiritual. What I discovered for myself is that spirituality is the journey of self-mastery. It is the quest of true self-discovery and all that it means: facing the parts of myself that were hard to look at and confronting all the deep unconscious programming that had shaped my world and perspective.

I found that spirituality ultimately leads to sovereignty: standing in our truth without swaying for other's opinions, even if they are well-intentioned. Sovereignty is a lifelong process, and spirituality is the practice that activates our being and shows us what we need to see to stand whole and free. Being spiritual *is* divine embodiment.

When we accept where and who we are, we come back to our center. It's always there, even if we don't feel good enough to be accepted yet. But the more we trust ourselves, the more we build that innate confidence to go farther than we could have ever imagined on the journey ahead. Spirituality is the desire to know oneself, deeply and truly.

Integrating All the Selves

When we begin to ask the question of "Who am I, really?" we go into deep soul territory. We go beyond all the thoughts, beliefs, and ideas that comprise the small self that is identified with the ego. We enter into the realm of the "Wise One" – or what I've been referring to as your divine authority. You might think of this as your "higher," "best," or "future" self; the one inside you that is already whole and complete, powerful, and at peace. It is the *Self*.

I dove into the scientific and esoteric equally, as I was in search of answers that would allow me to integrate every part of my life: the physical, emotional, mental, energetic, psychic, and divine aspects of my being that were seeking cohesion and expression. Through my research, I found myself reconciling a lot of the opposing beliefs I used to hold. I started seeing the mysticism in science, the spirit of the physical form, the gratitude within finance, the self-love within selfless service.

My journey taught me a lot about the multidimensional nature of existence. I now believe this word – multidimensional – describes every single person. What I mean by this is what we've been exploring: through the different perspectives and facets of being, we come to know and understand our complex and intricate nature, and how all those parts work together to serve the whole. We're operating on multiple levels of awareness at any given time: your heart is beating independently of your thinking about it, you are picking up data and sensory information from all your centers, you are thinking, emoting, reacting, and sensing with every inhale.

All these parts of you form a multitude: the qualities, attributes, abilities, preferences, and personas that comprise our selfhood. As you might have started to notice, your "self" isn't one thing: it's the integration and impulse of the many intersecting dimensions you occupy at any given time. Who you are with your lover or family unit might be very different from the way you show up at work or with friends. We have many "selves" that are operational at any given moment. Have you ever noticed yourself say, "A part of me" when you hold opposing or incongruent internal views on something?

Take a moment and reflect on different situations in your life. Notice who you are in relation to your colleagues, your family, your intimate partners, your friends. How do you show up in each space? Are there any parts of you that don't feel safe to show? Is there anywhere you hold back with certain people? If so, this is normal. We are navigating our inner universe constantly, and if you're like me, you've probably wondered at times which "self" is driving or what part of myself I'm shy about showing.

For instance, you might notice that sometimes your inner child is acting out and not dealing well with a difficult situation. Or, you might notice that you've been doing something for approval, rather than from inner alignment. Maybe you observe that when you're faced with a certain emotion or intensity – let's use anger as an example – that another part of you responds a certain way. Most of us are still learning about all the different selves we contain, even as adults. Ask yourself: are you the responsible one? The black sheep? The baby of the family? How do these different roles influence and impact you and others in your life? Are you in agreement with them or do you feel that sometimes you're not able to express yourself fully? Notice who is inhabiting your inner world and who comes forward in different situations and scenarios.

Archetypes can be a powerful wisdom tool for integrating all the different aspects of our being. Carl Jung coined the term *archetype* to represent a universally recognized thought-form, idea, primordial pattern, or image. While the term itself is modern, archetypes have been understood and utilized intentionally for centuries as a way of gaining a deeper understanding of unconscious behaviors and patterns.

The power of archetypes is most evident in the way they underlie and influence all of humanity across geography, race, religion, and culture. Jung deemed archetypes to be a collectively inherited unconscious idea or thought pattern that was present in individual psyches. Archetypes are in the Field, and we can access them through our transcendent intelligence; they are always present within and around us. Archetypes operate internally and are analogous, in a sense, to instinct: a thing or trait that motivates human behavior or creates an emotional response at some level. Even if you're not consciously working with archetypes, you have no doubt encountered them and are influenced by them. Consider: what do you think of when you hear the term Mother? What does a Mountain represent to you? Why does every culture have stories involving a Hero or Heroic Act? Why is Love universally cherished? Chances are, you have ideas about what each one of these things mean on a symbolic level. Such is the power of archetypes.

Archetypes helped me see that we all contain multiple aspects. Depending on the situation, I might step into my Warrior archetype if more assertive leadership is needed. In a moment that calls for nurturing and deep compassion, I might call on my inner Mother. If I am in a playful mood, I might be embodying my inner Child. I'm often on the lookout for my disempowering archetypes like the Victim or the Saboteur. We contain elements and aspects of many archetypes and embody different ones during various times in our life. We have some that stay with us our entire lives, and others who work with us for shorter periods. Using them consciously can help you tap into deep reservoirs of strength and resilience, for you will no doubt uncover aspects of yourself that you didn't realize existed!

Most people tend to rely on their strengths and expertise to create their success. While it's great to champion your strengths and play to them, not giving yourself the opportunity to explore other sides of yourself can inhibit your growth in the end. Humans are ever-changing and fluid, and throughout your life, you might find yourself inhabiting different archetypal aspects that serve you best in that moment. Work consciously with each archetype; even the ones you judge as negative or undesirable have important lessons.

In addition to archetypes, we also encounter the disembodied voices and inherited beliefs of our parents, early teachers and mentors, our community, and so forth. Everyone is impacted very early on by the cultural beliefs and systems in which they are raised. These unconscious ideas and beliefs imprint on our psyche early, leaving echoes that we remember for years to come. These imprints act as shadow selves; parts forgotten or purposely exiled, seeking the light of integration, compassion, and acceptance.

Becoming conscious is complicated! It might feel like a lot to awaken to all the parts of you that have a voice and want to be heard. One of the realizations that impacted me the most as I went through my awakening was the insight that I am not a person – I am a process. A person is akin to an object; a noun, a thing. I am not that. I am akin to a process; a verb, an action. I am constantly changing, unfolding, awakening, and evolving. Who I was five years ago is not the same woman that I am today. I have been different people at each part of my journey because with each step I uncovered a deeper aspect of my whole self. I was not seeking completion outside of myself, I was simply uncovering the whole truth of who was already there. I am pulling all these pieces, parts, and aspects of me back in, toward myself. In essence, I am putting myself back together. This is the ongoing practice of self-acceptance and self-mastery.

What this means is that there is no singular perfect self that we are trying to attain through self-mastery. This is not about cherry-picking the parts of yourself that feel the best to others and presenting only those. This is not about denying the parts of yourself that feel ugly, unloved, or too much. This is not about getting there. If you're a process, not a person, then there will always be something to learn, organize, optimize, or improve upon. You're not static or fixed in time, you are dynamic and exist relative to time. This is a realization that can be very liberating if you are ready to know yourself as you are: a constantly evolving creator, not a standard of static perfection.

The Serendipity of Surrender

For many years, I believed in working hard – indeed, toiling – to see the results I wanted. I was used to forcing perfection upon myself. I like to get things done, and I was used to doing it myself in order to deliver the necessary results. The idea of something coming easy, without the sweat, blood, and tears seemed ludicrous to me. Perhaps it was my conditioning, but I had a hard time believing that the life I wanted could be gentle, graceful, and easeful. I thought it was a child's wayward fantasy that anything would come *to* me, at my command. Images of wizards and witches may fill your vision, and they certainly did mine. "Nonsense!" My rational mind reprimanded me. "There's no such thing as magic."

Yet I started experiencing what could only be described as serendipity: that unexplainable sensation that everything was falling into place without my insistence, effort, or control. I noticed that the more I started to align with myself and honor my inner authority, the less I struggled. The synchronicities were uncanny, which caused me to raise my skeptical eyebrow. My experience was defying everything I knew to be true – up until now.

Intention is a command and when it is channeled through coherence, it calls forward its aligned manifestation. As we've been saying, intuition emerges in the senses and it's up to us to pay attention and translate the signs.

This is your invitation to start noticing what's happening in your body, mind, and spirit if you haven't been actively observing already. It's a good opportunity to look around your world and notice: What has your body been communicating to you if you were to truly listen? What does your gut say about the choices you've been making? Do you feel a rush or a depletion of energy when considering a new direction? Does your mind interject with reruns of negative narratives? How does your heart feel about the situations and people who are present in your world?

After the excruciating heartbreak of Barrington's passing, I was in a liminal state for months. I tried to go about my days as the lonely silence permeated our home and my heart. After almost a year, I started to peruse dog rescues, slowly reacquainting myself with the idea of having another furry soul by my side. After a few months, I found one. Duke was on the East Coast and had a number of health problems, but I didn't care. "The one who can't breathe *and* can't walk?!" Andrew asked. My application was denied. I wasn't surprised.

I decided to reach out to the same rescue organization where we had adopted Barrington and let them know I was ready to adopt again. Shortly after, a striking and sad dog appeared on their feed: Ambrose was skin and bones from starvation, his head cracked and broken from outdoor exposure, and didn't have a single hair on his body due to uncontrolled mange. His owner had kept him in the backyard and was rarely home. He was a sight: broken in body but not in spirit. He had yellow eyes, like Barrington. However, Ambrose was one of the more popular dogs on the rescue's feed and many had expressed interest in adopting him when he was fully healed, which was months away.

A week later the rescue called to let me know that a puppy in Seattle had been rescued by a good Samaritan from a backyard breeder and named her Petal. I coordinated directly with the woman and booked my flight to Seattle to pick up Petal. Less than 24 hours before my departure, I received a text from the woman letting me know she was keeping the dog. I was devastated, dismayed, and heartbroken. Mainly, I was frustrated. I couldn't understand. *Why is this happening?* Andrew and I had prepared our home and our hearts for this puppy – we had even pre-printed her name tag. The unease I had felt throughout the coordination with the puppy's rescuer surfaced again. I had had a feeling something would go awry. But there's a good end to this story, for the next day the owner of the rescue called asked if we would like to foster Ambrose. We took him in, cared for him, and began nursing him back to health. After 6 weeks, we adopted him. As I was filling out the adoption paperwork, I noticed the documents stating his name as it had been given to him by his original owner: Duke.

Let me ask you: What has shown up for you when you needed it most? What twists and turns have you been on that seemed doomed but turned out in the end? At what point did you trust? At what point did you give up? When did you surrender?

Using your intuition is about becoming an avid observer of your reality. This can make the world feel like an adventure as you start to tune into the subtle languages of your intuition speaking through situations in your life to you. Learning to trust more and more in your intuition is a form of surrender. You start to let go of the controlling ideas and actions that dominate your world and start to pay more attention to what life is presenting you. You might just find that it feels like magic.

Making Better Decisions

When you can harness your intuition and understand how to effectively utilize it, you open the door to better decision-making. Why? Because you question yourself less. Doubt is the opposite of inner authority. It leads you to second guess and over analyze situations, fretting and worrying rather than making an empowered decision that you trust. In its purest form, intuition is the answer you already know to be true for you. Intuition is efficient.

Intuition might have seemed "woo" at one point, but by now you're hopefully starting to see the potency of your productive intuition. When you have the ability to access all parts of yourself, you gain access to the information each part holds, too. Working with your intuition can help guide you more effectively than your go-to strategies, for you are working with an extremely powerful and interconnected set of intelligences.

Intuition cuts through the noise: thoughts, worries, doubts, rumination, emotions, biases, and what-ifs. The brain can be tricked and manipulated in many ways, but your intuition can't, for it exists outside your rational experience. Rather, it speaks through your senses and perceptions to cohere critical data points. Your experience informs your intuition, certainly, but it's the intuition that helps you sort through all the information to arrive at the data and the solution that matters most. For example, you might find yourself faced with a difficult decision in business. Your expertise might support you in clarifying and understanding the problem you're navigating, yet sometimes you just "know." Your higher mind can get to the real insight immediately and "pop" it forward because it's integrated the necessary information so effectively. You don't even need to think about it.

One personal practice that opened up my intuition in an unexpected way: learning how to listen. This sounds simple, and yet it's incredible how often most people aren't really listening – they're just preparing what to say next. There is a difference. Now, when I listen to people, I can feel myself more available to all the information they're sharing: what they're saying and what they're not saying, body language, the energy in the exchange, and so on. I let go of the small, thinking mind and allow my higher mind to synthesize, pattern, and process while I intently and genuinely focus on the other person. In other words, I am fully present. When I let go of the need to reply, have an opinion, or be right in my response, I find that I receive much deeper intuitive hits of insight that I'm better equipped to communicate to the person in the moment. This enhances every interaction because the exchange is heart-centered, attuned, and deeply resonant.

If you're someone who struggles to stay focused in conversation, do your best to slow down and get centered before diving deep with someone. See what information or insights emerge as you slow down your own mind and listen. What ideas, questions, or responses emerge? What information "lands" in your body and feels true? Do you receive any "downloads" or instant aha's? How does this allow you to be better in your interactions and role?

Discernment is the key to taking action on the information you receive. It's important to check in and ask yourself: Is this information truly responding to this person? Or, do I feel the need to validate/affirm/please in order to generate a certain response? Am I leading with ego or projecting onto this person? These kinds of internal probing questions can help you determine the best information to share in reflection. Intuition helps you access your internal intelligence centers; discernment helps you make the best action plan with the data.

Unlocking Visionary Creativity

The most celebrated visionaries have been deeply connected to their inner authority and intuition. This ability allowed them to "see" into the future, calling forward the inspirational ideas, revered images, and creative expressions of the era.

If you consider yourself a visionary, then it's essential to develop your connection to your intuition, for this is where your true power and potential live. What I've found is that as I've cultivated my intuition, I was better able to identify potential and creative capability in others as well. I've always had a good sense of trends and could pinpoint what would be successful in the future. When I did intellectual property development and scouting, I was always working on the bleeding edge of "What's Next?" I started a global art licensing business with my sister, Camilla, at the start of the great recession in 2008. We made the controversial decision to grow an independent artist brand during an economic downtown. We leveraged social media, in its earliest days, to grow her audience before most people knew how to use Twitter, and before these platforms became essential to business growth. Camilla quickly became a leading artist-entrepreneur at a time when everyone said it wasn't possible. We proved it was possible, and she's still thriving today.

When I met early employees of Uber in 2011 and they showed me the app on the phone, I had a strong hit. I'd never seen anything like it, but I intuitively knew they were on to something. Similarly, I immediately understood that coworking was going to change the way entrepreneurs, startups, and independent creators would collaborate when I moved to Silicon Beach in 2012 and found myself working out of a small, independent, co-working space. After working on several Kickstarter projects, I intuited the potential of crowdfunding to influence and shape the real estate industry in 2013. For a few months, I worked to understand how I might leverage coworking and crowdfunding trends to buy a multi-million-dollar house on the canals in Venice Beach, but I wasn't able to put the model together. Now, large boutique homes in Venice are exclusive co-working spaces for hip locals.

I share this because at the time I wouldn't have called myself intuitive – or visionary – or creative! I played down this incredible source of powerful inspiration, excitement, and information that was constantly and clearly speaking to me. I didn't recognize what was happening at first: my intuition was showing me an abundance of opportunities that I could choose to look further into, to focus on, to dedicate myself to. While I didn't take action on every intuitive insight or visionary idea, I did end up following through on one – real estate crowdfunding.

In my attempt to buy that beautiful home on the canals and monetize it through a coworking model, I ended up smack in the middle of the early stages of real estate crowdfunding. A handful of companies had emerged to provide an online platform for connecting investors seeking real estate investments with companies seeking investment capital to buy, renovate, lease-up, and manage buildings such as large apartments, or to invest in the underlying debt (mortgages) of fix-and-flip builders. After going to one of the first real estate crowdfunding conferences, I met the founders of one such company and joined the team as their Chief Marketing Officer. To say that the next three years were a wild ride is an understatement.

I was leveraging my background in finance and investing, my entrepreneurial spirit, my love of the bleeding edge of technology, and my visionary intuition to build and promote not only the company but also the opportunity of crowdfunding itself. Never before had it been possible for "regular people" to invest in this type of real estate. It democratized the ability for more people to build wealth with the most proven wealth-building tool on the planet – real estate. During those years, I cultivated a new career, network, knowledgebase, and skillset that perfectly married my abilities, passions, and interests.

Visionaries, innovators, creators, artists, inventors, futurists, opportunists: anyone driving the future is using their intuition to sense what's next and following up through empowered action. We are all visionaries to some extent. When we operate at our most expansive capacity we embody the word *genius* in its fullest expression: an inspired ability to see beyond what exists. Intuition and intellect work hand in hand, and together they operate as a superpower that has demonstrated time and time again that it will change the world.

Reflection Questions:

1. Reflect on a time when you had a psychic hit about something or someone. How did you react? Did you feel excited or ashamed? How did you treat this psychic ability?

____

____

____

____

2. Reflect on a time when you had a visionary or innovative idea. It came out of nowhere but you knew that it was valid. Did you follow up on the idea? What happened?

____

____

____

____

3. What parts of me do I hold back? Who do I hold back from, or in which situations do I hold back? What parts of myself am I most comfortable embodying? Which parts do I reject?

____

____

____

____

Actionable Practices:

1. Start keeping an eye out for signs and synchronic-
    ities in your world. How is your intuition commu-
    nicating with you? What are you noticing or paying
    attention to lately?

---

2. Practice the *Who Am I?* self-inquiry and enlight-
    enment meditation by Ramana Maharshi, which is
    briefly described here:

a. At the moment a thought arises, ask, "to whom did
    this (thought) rise?" The mind will answer, "to me."
    At that point, ask, *"who am I?"*

---

b. The mind is said to turn back (to Self) to answer
    the question and, with repeated practice, the mind
    gains comfort, ability, and power to abide in its
    Source.

---

3. Working with your Defining Moment again, journal as you contemplate the following:

a. Zoom out and reflect on the situation. As best as you can, observe every detail with as much neutrality as possible. Take the perspective of the Wise One.

____

____

____

____

b. Looking back, what is the overall message, knowledge, or wisdom that you gained from this experience?

____

____

____

____

Go Deeper:

1. *Sacred Contracts* by Caroline Myss

2. *Astrology, Psychology and the Four Elements* by Stephen Arroyo, M.A.

3. *The Llewellyn Complete Book of Psychic Empowerment* by Carl Llewellyn Weschke & Joe H. Slate, PH.D.

CHAPTER 8

New M&A — Meaning & Alignment

Mantra:

I am aligned with my inner divine authority.

I am merged with my source of meaning.

I am allied to my highest potential. My life is meaningful.

My life is aligned with my inner values and principles.

I am my own ally.

Keywords:

Intention, Signal, Frequency, Channel,

Transmission, Anchor, Direction

Through this book, you have been learning some powerful ways to develop self-mastery. We are now moving into full integration through practices of applied embodiment. Here, you will begin to work on the soul-level as you integrate the teachings and tools of the previous chapters.

This chapter will illuminate the inner drivers of your alignment process and your embodied evolution. You will connect to your divine authority through your inner landscape; uncovering your meaning, purpose, values, principles, and desires through the exercises and insights ahead. At this point, you should be feeling more confident in your intuitive nature and more connected to your power source. I hope that you are excited to work more deeply with this part of yourself and that you are feeling empowered by the insights and progress you've made so far.

You are at a pivotal moment in your transformation process, and this is no small feat. You've awakened your *transcendent perceptual faculties* and gained more access to your inner divine authority. You have no doubt opened and expanded yourself, and now you might be wondering what to do with this information and how to best integrate it into your daily life.

The transmissions and practices contained within this book are designed to shake stuff loose and dissolve illusions that are not serving you in your journey. You might be feeling lighter, excited, more confident, and enjoying more clarity in your daily life. Due to the nature of the energetic realignment that you're invested in, you might also be feeling destabilized, ungrounded, or like you're still putting all the pieces back together. Perhaps a combination of all of the above!

What's happening is that underneath the surface, you have been refining who you are. You've been releasing many outdated concepts of self, calcified emotions that were magnetizing what you didn't want, past hurts that kept you from your present power, and doubts about your worthiness to be magical and deserving of serendipity! You are still immersed in your process and while you have seen progress, it will take time for everything to land, take root, and work consistently. You've been awakening your sovereign being – and you've *just* started stretching.

This chapter is designed to establish and anchor new foundations of your sovereignty. This chapter is designed for you to coalesce what before seemed separate and to support your integration with ease and grace.

If I'm an expert at anything, it's impatience. I've been known to jump the gun, dive headfirst into the deep end, or play with a new tool without reading the instructions. This is sometimes fun, other times distressing, and always informative of my potential and my limits. I have found that I learn best by taking my visionary ideas and explorations and grounding them through effective practices that deliver real results.

A lot of trial and error is involved with the transformational journey and evolutionary process. You may find yourself going down a rabbit hole to suddenly realize you're not "feeling it," or that you don't need as much support in one area because you already feel strong there. This is totally, completely, okay – and even something to be celebrated! There is no right or wrong direction, no midterm, and no final exam. No one is going to jump out from behind the bush to trip you up. There is no such thing as lost time or wasted research or a useless escapade when it comes to understanding how your intuitive nature, transcendent intelligence, and inner authority interact with you.

When I first started going through the awakening process, I imagined that I had to give up my "real life:" my financial career and my place in society. I eschewed materialism and, embarrassingly, judged my world for being a left-brain, matrix-enslavement culture of evil white men. Of course, now I understand how harmful that line of judgmental reasoning is, and at the time, I thought everything about *me* was wrong because that had been my unconscious understanding of the World and I operated within it – asleep and unknowing. Like an iceberg, I had only been focused on the small portion of what was visible above the waterline, when the bulk, the breadth, and the depth of who I truly am was beneath the surface.

I didn't know how to communicate to Andrew that I was being destroyed from the inside out, while simultaneously feeling more myself than ever. I thought for sure I would lose him; he would think I was crazy, reject me, and inevitably I would have to banish myself to some mountaintop monastery. Alas, I found my way back to my center. Along the way, I sat through the discomfort of expressing emotions and describing experiences that I had no sufficient language for, I reluctantly surrendered to what was happening, and ultimately trusted both Andrew and those who cared for and supported me.

I wrote this book to show that it was *not* impossible to have a spiritual awakening and still keep my life running while enjoying success in the material world. I realized that my divine authority wasn't just something I tapped into on my meditation cushion; it was the embodied application of the wisdom I was receiving.

This wisdom is present in every moment of my life – from a call with a potential investor to a BBQ with my neighbor. The wisdom is present in moments I would otherwise judge as not spiritual because I'm not acting particularly enlightened. Let me just say this: enlightenment and spirituality aren't good vibes only. You'll fly into a rage, you'll project, you'll judge, you'll be embarrassed by the thoughts that enter your head. Every day, maybe multiple times a day. This is all spiritual. Your shadow is spiritual. Your ego is spiritual. Your cellulite is spiritual. And your worst days are spiritual. Trust that whatever comes up is exactly what you're meant to work with, transmute, and heal. This is the work of self-mastery.

So, let's begin the work of embodiment.

For business-minded people, it can be helpful to think of the work we're doing in this chapter as "mergers and acquisitions for self-mastery" – except M&A now stands for Meaning and Alignment. You're bringing all the parts together and consolidating them into a more powerful entity that can resource itself more effectively. Meaning and alignment operate in the same way: they help us cohere and make sense of the information so that we have a clear understanding of how to apply it in our daily life. Constructing meaning for yourself is like building the foundations of a building; coming into alignment is the equivalent of the structures that support your strength and reach. This brings about growth, expansion, and enhanced efficiencies.

Just like a merger inevitably results in some internal chaos, aligning to your inner authority is a restructuring that can make you feel shaky before you feel solid. This is because you are in a deep re-patterning of your internal beliefs, stories, programs, identities, and emotions. Crafting meaning and coming into alignment is critical for our self-actualization and self-mastery, regardless of how challenging we find it. When we articulate and construct systems that align to our values, we replace old unconscious programs with new patterns sourced from our divine authority.

When we start to engage with our inner work at this level, it becomes less about solving all the problems and more about coming from total alignment in everything we do. That changes the nature of our engagement with the external world. When things feel "against" us, it's easy to feel disempowered by what life hands us. But when we start to see our life through our "soul values," we unlock the majesty inside each moment.

What is Meaningful, Really?

We are all seeking meaning on some level. Underneath the striving, wishing, chasing, and wanting, we are all seeking meaning. We are looking for what matters, what's important, what is necessary for us to feel whole. Yet if we are not connected to ourselves, nothing we find outside us will matter. The only meaning that will satisfy is the one that is found inside.

When we turn our attention, intention, and focus toward ourselves and what defines our drives, we come to rest on an expansive shore of meaning. Our world opens up and becomes oceanic, for we are tapping into an infinite and self-filling reservoir of power.

Many of us are asked to define our "why" in life. The "why" can be illuminating, but if it's not connected to your inner values then it isn't going to serve you in the long run. You can say you want to solve world hunger, but if you don't value service or collaboration or the work necessary to build a legacy organization, then the why doesn't matter so much. That's why it's important to investigate and explore our underlying motives: so we can anchor into the heart of our purpose and use our inner authority to serve it.

My awakening has taught me many things, one of the most important being how I related to myself through my career path. I struggled to understand how I could be both practical and esoteric, why I was working in real estate during the day but researching astrology in the evenings. I wondered if I was in the right place *many* times. At a certain point, I realized that it's not what I do but why I'm doing it, where it connects to my values, and how I show up for the process at hand. I could be a fintech executive *and* bring my inner alignment into the work I did because they benefitted each other in the end. Finally, I felt whole.

Sometimes it takes time to uncover what gives our lives real meaning. The actual content of our lives can occasionally get conflated with the consuming distractions within it. We must become better at discerning what is truly necessary and what is only urgent. Most of us are constantly bombarded with messages telling us who to be and what to do. The decisions, however, are ours, as is the decision about *how* we want to be. The underlying truth of something can be a bit harder to see underneath all the noise. Yet this is why we take the time to ask "What matters most to me? What do I truly value? Why am I doing this?" and "Why is this meaningful?"

Granted, sometimes we just want that ice cream and a self-inquiry process isn't necessary! However, if you're making big decisions without checking in, that's more worrisome. Now, when I'm invited to engage or invest time in something, I inquire into the underlying meaning several times, in concentric spirals or layers. You'll start to see that the more you ask the simple question of "Why is this meaningful?" your answer starts to shift and go deeper. With each answer, ask again, "Why is *that* meaningful? Why does *that* matter?" At the bottom, when you can no longer answer the question of why something is meaningful any differently, you'll see your core driving incentives, values, and motivations. You find your deep, driving desire, which is the meaning you seek.

True, there will be things we are asked or are required to do in life that we don't agree nor align with. Sometimes we get bored or tired or frustrated and the meaning fails to motivate us as it once did. Stresses exist, yet we have the power to shift our response through noticing, redirecting, and reframing our attention. Meaning is available at every moment.

There is a parable about two stonemasons. Each is laboriously carving a stone. When asked, one says his work is to simply carve a stone. However, the other states that he's building a cathedral. This simple story illustrates the power of how we create meaning when we are faced with the more tedious and tiresome details of our life's work. There are many ways to work with the energies that feel less welcome, and the biggest shift you can make is in your perspective and embodied presence. Can you find even just a little bit of joy in what you label a tedious chore? Can you tap a sense of purpose or contribution in doing something that doesn't directly benefit you? What if you approached the mundane with inspiration?

Working from home and having obsessive-compulsive tendencies, I notice everything dirty and out of place. I used to find myself constantly doing house chores and getting frustrated because I felt less productive in my career work. I was telling myself that I should be "working" or that Andrew should be doing more, etc. Then one day I realized that 1) I was proactively choosing to do those tasks, and, 2) those tasks were opportunities to take breaks, move around *and* be productive around the house.

When I stopped actively running my anger narrative, I realized that these tasks helped to clear my mind. In fact, they served an important purpose in sifting through thoughts, problems, and ideas and I would often get the answers or intuitive hits while I was busy folding laundry or sweeping floors. I often emerged feeling calmer and oddly satisfied. I found meaning and purpose in my actions, and this helped me feel good about my process.

With this awareness, I went deeper, and now proactively walk away from work when I reach a point where I can no longer take it forward, instead of forcing myself to keep going. Small, subtle shifts like this empower a more productive process with less self-recrimination and a lot more energy. I feel clearer and lighter. Plus, it feels great to have a clean, tidy house!

Investigating your internal world is brave and necessary. Taking the time to understand what intentions you're bringing to the table will help you show up in more empowered, actionable ways. This leads to a radical sense of personal accountability. Rather than be surprised and disempowered when your unconscious actions sabotage your intentions, you are stepping into conscious integrity and alignment.

You can start to shift into your empowered creator state at any time. We make sense of our world by assigning meaning to everything we encounter. Even the things you have decided are bad. You just don't realize this in the moment, but you have the ability to redefine the meaning of anything that doesn't work for you. So even if things feel out of control outside you, you can still choose your inner state. Are you going to carve a stone or build a cathedral?

When Success Becomes Clear

The more you can interrogate and examine your response to perceived challenges, the more empowered you become. For example, let's say you get passed up for a promotion. What does that mean for you? How do you take that news? Do you run away with negativity and tell yourself that you're unworthy, that you didn't work hard enough, that you shouldn't have gotten your hopes up? Do you blame it on someone instead of taking responsibility? Do you see it as a hidden gift? What meaning did you assign the promotion to prove your worth? Anytime you find yourself wanting to insert an old storyline (i.e. "I'm not good enough" or "This is what I deserve for stepping outside my lane"), try reframing your limiting narrative into one that feels more expansive and supportive. You might find that when you stop subscribing to these ideas, you actually uncover what matters to you now.

Shortly after leaving the real estate crowdfunding startup I helped create, I took on an even higher profile executive-level position for a company in the fintech space. My intuition warned me something was off. My ego, on the other hand, was all about it. Despite my better inner judgment, I took the position. I made valuable contributions and believed in the company's future, but I felt dissonance and exhaustion. The constant, subtle anxiety I felt eclipsed my enthusiasm and conviction. It became clear that although I was giving my best, somehow I felt thwarted in the bigger contribution and meaning I was seeking from this role. After evaluating the many subtle indications and obvious signs, I knew: I needed to pursue my path. Unbeknownst to me at the time, that path wasn't a career path; it was the deepening of my awakening process that was already underway, and kicked off the even more intense "dark night of the soul."

This was the period I referenced in earlier chapters when I experienced depression, burnout, hopelessness, and a sense of loss – financial, career direction, and identity. But, it wasn't all lost. That's not how it works. Trust, surrender, and alignment are how it works. Months into what felt like an interminable quagmire, and 3 days after I had a full-blown breakdown about my predicament, I received a call from one of the founders of a boutique real estate investment firm. I had met this group shortly after I left the crowdfunding company. I respected their approach to the business and we shared the same values, morals, and sense of integrity, honor, and servant leadership. Over the years, I had gladly provided insights, referrals, and advice whenever I could. I agreed to meet, expecting to catch up on the usual things: projects, business, personal endeavors. Instead, they asked if I would join as a partner in the firm. That call may have been surprising to my rational mind, but my inner authority knew better.

About a year after joining this firm, I was tapped for a CEO position for a company in the wellness sector. I was curiously excited about this opportunity, and my ego puffed up a little. I noticed but was determined not to let it get the best of me –or make the same mistakes again. This time, alongside my due diligence regarding the role, company, and opportunity, I did a deep internal inquiry. I explored the meaning I was assigning to the role and the story I was telling myself. I looked at where it was or wasn't aligned with my values. Even though I did value the legacy and prestige that came with being a CEO in a space I am passionate about, the opportunity came with a strong feeling that left me uncomfortable. My intuition was pinging.

My takeaways from the conversation with my inner authority were profound. I realized that I already had a lot of satisfaction in my existing role and lifestyle – so much so that I realized something profound: I finally had everything I said I wanted back when I was 18 and decided to pursue a career in professional investing. I had been so busy chasing success that I didn't stop to acknowledge that I already had it by my own definitions!

Rather than turning down the role directly, I entered into a lengthy conversation with the founder of the wellness company. Together we arrived at a place that felt empowered, productive, and deeply human. We were able to connect and get to a place of truth and understanding that wasn't based on me selling myself or my skill set. I stood in my worth and showed up in service to what was best for me, and that influenced the direction of my follow-up conversation with the founder. I found myself more able to advocate for myself from a place of worth and recognition. Since that day, I've turned my attention and conviction toward the business and the partners with whom I am deeply aligned. In the 12 months following the "CEO conversation," we doubled revenue and beat all projections for the year, setting the company on a new growth trajectory. I found a deeper sense of peace and contentment where I was, and this translated itself into a new stability in all areas of my life. I already had everything I was looking for, there was no more need to strive.

The Power of Personal Values

When most people describe themselves, they default to their role, title, or job function. They tell you what they *do*, not who they *are*. It seems to be a difficult question for people to answer. I've found that a great way to approach the question from a place of empowered worth is to answer by stating my values: I value relationships. I value integrity. I value authenticity. I value freedom. I value equality. I value collaboration. I value self-empowerment. I value personal responsibility. I value contemplation, reflection, and self-inquiry. I value stillness and peace. I value learning. I value creativity. I value hard work. I value financial stability.

Values are helpful tools because they make clear where we are investing our time. Take a look at your world, because what you value surrounds you. If you don't like what your situation or surroundings look like, then it's a powerful time to reflect on and rewrite your core values. Some values we hold for an entire lifetime, others we let go of as we shift and evolve. Sometimes we might find that we think we value something, only to realize later we don't. This happens a lot with money and meaning. One friend recently shared with me that she is more interested in creating meaning, purpose, and impact than about making boatloads of money. Money can feel like an empty success for some, while for others it can facilitate the meaningful life they seek. It isn't a question of whether or not you are deserving of wealth. Wealth is many things, not just money. The real question is: "What do you value?" and secondarily, "What does wealth mean to you?"

Discerning the values you hold dear in life empowers you to boldly state, intentionally manifest, and take action toward your deep driving desires. Knowing and aligning to your values is what makes lasting change possible. When we are maintaining a false identity or behaviors to please others or entertain concepts of success, happiness, or self-worth that don't serve our growth, then we compromise the integrity of our larger reality. We don't give ourselves the opportunity to experience life as we actually want it – and of course, we suffer because we're misaligned with what matters to us. You can choose otherwise. You can choose to align your actions and your outer reality to your values. This is self-empowerment 101.

Do an inventory of your values related to the following: material needs, security, sexuality; relationships, family, community; self-worth, career, and purpose; love, abundance, and prosperity; self-expression, communication, and creativity; spirituality, nature, and humanity. Observe what values intersect or appear multiple times. Is there a larger underlying value that applies to different areas of your life? Can you distill all your values into 1-5 core words?

What should be clear at the end of this exercise is how you desire your life to feel meaningful and whether or not you are living in alignment with that truth or not. Are you using up all your time managing relationships that drain you? Are you holding onto things that aren't good for you? Are you doing things that get you external validation but leave you feeling empty inside? Does checking that one box make your stomach sink or your heart break?

If these questions bring up shame, guilt, blame, or judgment, let those thoughts and emotions go; let them come up, and flow out. You need them less than you need the clarity that you're gaining! You're carving a clear path to the alignment of your values, which will help you take the most direct route to your deep driving desires. Be inspired by the work you are doing, and the movement generated by the inquiry and self-examination. Get into your heart space, find coherence, and breathe. After all: you are clearing the way for what you really want to come in.

Authority Requires Alignment

We can't actualize inner authority without alignment. We can describe it, reflect on it and get glimpses of it on certain occasions, but if we are not connected to our authority, then it's harder for the full experience of truth to come through. This can lead to feelings of frustration and doubt, or even a sense of betrayal by life itself if things are really challenging. Occasionally, we *all* wobble off-center. But unless we take the necessary actions to course correct, we'll wander off the path and wind up somewhere else.

What I've noticed in this kind of work is that the transformation process isn't linear. Certain areas in our lives will see immediate shifts and restructuring, others will take more time and patience. Sometimes, what worked before will stop being as effective. When that happens, it's a good sign that we've come out of alignment and need to get back into our center before we take another step. This is usually because our ego, rather than our inner authority, is operational.

Waking up isn't a direct path – nor is it easy to follow at all times. Alignment is a lifetime practice that takes you deeper into your true nature. Alignment is when our actions emerge from our pure intentions, not from ego ploys. Productivity describes the clarity that comes internally when the channels between our centers are open and clear, making it easier to receive insights as they arise.

What are we aligning to, exactly? Inner authority is derived from our personal meaning, values, and desires, for each informs and drives the others. Our desires come from the heart and often come with great feelings or emotions attached to them. They are deep wishes that we are expressing to others or ourselves in order to have them fulfilled. Whether we are granted an answer to our wish or must co-create it ourselves, a desire is something we act upon with the full support of our divine authority.

There is an important distinction to illuminate between desires and wants. We can want five cookies, but we might desire to feel satiated and satisfied. The want is the means to the end, whereas the desire is the beginning expression, the urge itself. A desire feels intentional and empowering, whereas want often implies lack. In fact, the dictionary definition of want *is* lack. When we want for something, we are longing for that which we are not receiving. When we state we want something, we're starting from the energetic position of not having it, we're already behind the starting line.

Desire is the opposite of that feeling. Desire is a deep urge to make something real; it implies it is already there and available, and with the right intention, that desire is easily fulfilled.

How often do you express your desires in terms of wants, or even needs? How often do you acknowledge your own desires to yourself? Does it feel uncomfortable to name your desires or describe them? Try replacing "I want..." with "I desire..." and see what happens. You might find that your reframe changes the energetics of the exchange instantly.

The Impact of Alignment

When we get into alignment with our core desires, it becomes easier to see our deep truth with greater clarity and compassion. This creates a domino effect in our system. Suddenly, we see the things that were hidden inside our previous confusion: namely, our principles, purpose, magnetism, and personal power.

Principles offer an expanded perspective on how to restructure our inner landscape once we've cleared away the unconscious programming and patterns that were dominating our attention and energy. A principle is a fundamental truth or position, a foundation of reasoning that underlies your opinions and helps you live a life consistent with your values. Ask yourself: What forms the foundation of your beliefs? What is your baseline approach to life? Do you question the easy quips such as "How you do one thing is how you do anything"? Does that ring true for you? What do you believe are the fundamental ingredients for success or happiness? Ray Dalio, the famed CEO of the worlds' biggest hedge fund, Bridgewater, is known for his outspoken views on how capitalism needs to change as well as the powerful principles he's distilled about business and life. For example: "Own Your Outcomes" or "Embrace Reality and Deal With It." Principles inspire in their simplicity. Principles are universal and foundational. With self-reflection, you'll align to your principles with greater awareness.

Humans seek purpose just as much as they seek meaning. We love to inquire as to why we are here and what that means. Purpose is challenging to define but one of the easiest things to embody once it clicks, for it's truly about being who we already are. It is presence in action. It's about living into our fullest self, whatever that looks like. Purpose emerges from relaxing into ourselves, not forcing an outcome or end point that we think is valuable, impactful, or worth it. Purpose is natural, inherent, organic. It arises if we let go of identifying with our job, our role, our status, or our things. Purpose is not a moving target that we chase; nor is it anything we get, achieve, or attain. Being purposeful means that we have infused real meaning into the work, regardless of what activity we are involved in. One can be purposeful in the grocery store just as one can be purposeful in saving the world.

Having purpose is important because it is intrinsically connected to our sense of wellbeing. A study in Japan found that adults who reported having *ikigai*—a Japanese term meaning "a reason for being" or "a source of value in one's life or the things that make one's life worthwhile"—often lived at least seven years longer than those without *ikigai*. These studies have been replicated in America and have found similar results: purpose leads to a greater sense of fulfillment, prosperity, happiness, and meaning. To do anything intentionally automatically starts to invest meaning into it, creating a rewarding experience for all involved.

Many people operate from lack every day. We're always running out of time, out of energy, out of money, out of motivation. We've been programmed to think that we lack magic and so we work tirelessly to prove our worth to ourselves and each other. When that happens, it feels like abundance is a place outside of us, for we are depleting our reservoirs through actions rather than replenishing them. Yet we are naturally magnetic, calling toward us that which we need to evolve and grow stronger. Manifestation is a natural skill of an aligned human. We only need to clear the debris and accrued gunk out of our system to experience the ease and abundance of our innate vitality in action.

Abundance is a natural state of being. Abundance is our birthright because abundance is inherent in the way Nature operates. Nature is abundant in every way! It is our culture and societal conditions that have trained us to believe otherwise. It is greed that creates the illusion of lack and spurs actions that create the imbalances that have affected so many people, unjustly.

Greed is a human trait, which stems from fear and mistrust and a belief in scarcity. As with any false belief, it too can be turned around, dissolved, and let go. When we do the work of aligning to abundance within, we are doing work for the whole of humanity. We're seeing the dire consequences of greed unhinged – but don't let that discourage you. As someone who has worked for years to clear false ideas of lack and scarcity, I know that anyone can access the inherent abundance within and manifest it externally as well. Take a moment now to feel abundant. Can you find alignment with it? If not, what is blocking it? What thoughts, memories, or emotions come up? Getting into alignment with abundance as a birthright is a powerful foundational practice of sovereignty.

Finally, personal power manifests when we have access to all our intelligence centers. That gives us the ability to tap into all the information that is available to us at any given time; creating the experience of expanded potential. It should be empowering to you to know that you have a wealth of knowledge, wisdom, and insight that already exists, and all you have to do is tap into it.

What does being out of alignment feel like? It feels similar to what you would expect: a sense of dissonance and self-doubt, a lack of trust, feelings of chaos both internally and externally, frustration, lack of coherence and clarity. When we feel off-kilter in these ways, we are experiencing the wobbly feeling that occurs when we go off-center. Acknowledging your needs on the internal layers allows you to bring your external world into greater coherence. It may mean making some difficult choices in your work, relationships, or time investments – yet ultimately, having clear values defines who we are in our daily choices and actions.

My friend, international author and speaker Bronwen Sciortino, recently shared her story of listening to her intuition and finding alignment during important contract negotiations. When the negotiations started going sideways she got a sudden jolt in her body and immediately recognized it. Her intuition was telling her something wasn't right and that she needed to stop and take the time to have a detailed look rather than continue going through the motions. She had to deeply inspect *what* she was doing, *how* she was doing it, and most importantly *why* she was doing it. Bronwen discovered that she was spending time on things she didn't enjoy, but that she was good at. These things were extracting her energy and enthusiasm, leaving her feeling drained. When she sat with the truth and asked what felt aligned, she realized that not only did she not want to be doing certain things anymore, but that these things comprised the bulk of the contract she was negotiating! With that clarity, she completely changed the focus of the conversation and started the negotiations again, which led to new terms and a contract full of things she wants to be doing. She set her own terms. In turn, she says that she has more energy, more focus, and more time because she's realigned her life with what matters to her.

My Meaning Making

After a lifetime chasing ideals and definitions of wealth, health, happiness, and success that I thought were right because society told me so, I woke up to my real answer. I woke up to *all* the answers. It turns out that they weren't in the executive suite, or in my stock portfolio, or in size 2 jeans. My answers were definitely not inside others' expectations or in comparing and competing with the world around me.

My answers were not in my identities or my job description. They didn't exist in all the "shoulds" that sprinkled my life. The search for meaning never took me anywhere but deeper inside myself, for all the answers I needed were there.

It took me countless lessons, challenges, and personal struggles. It took breakdowns and breakthroughs and moments of shaking my fist at the heavens. It turns out that finding myself required the total destruction of who I thought I was – *several* times.

Through self-inquiry, meditation, reflection, ritual, and a lot of excavating, I finally found my soul. It was buried under my ego. This part of me that couldn't hide the truth was also hiding from me because I hadn't bothered to listen to its needs. It was time to go within, and from there I started my evolutionary process of self-inquiry.

What I uncovered was a connection to myself that was immovable, unshakeable, and centered. The part of me that had nothing to fear because it was certain of what needed to be done.

I began to question everything. Nothing was sacred anymore, no area of my investigation was out of bounds. The more I examined my motivations, illusions, and delusions, the more I began to trust myself. Because in looking at all the pieces of myself I was connecting to the whole me.

In a sense, I came home to myself: to the curious, mischievous, fiery, wise, and innocent self that I buried so long ago.

I came back to my heart and my emotions. I came back to loving my body, managing my energy, and mastering my mind. I returned to my eternal truth and I started living there wholly. I started to feel more resonant, embodied, and present in my life. I felt more satisfaction being myself than I had in the previous years of striving for influence, authority, and external affirmations. In my search for meaning, I found a path that served my evolutionary impulse.

Though unique to this person named AdaPia, my story is not just mine. Like myths, each of us carries a deep wisdom that has existed since the dawn of humanity. This story of the soul is a narrative we recognize in some way, shape, or form, for it is a very human story. We are all on the path learning how to become freer, more "me." Each of us is the main character and the hero.

In my journey, I found a level of freedom I did not know was possible. I learned how to reconnect with my deep driving desires and to manifest the kind of meaning that made me feel alive where it truly matters. I learned how to understand the signals I was receiving – and also, more importantly, the ones I was ignoring. I learned how to harness the immense power within me to create a fulfilling life on my own terms. I learned the importance of honoring myself.

I learned the power of words and the meaning we assign to them. I learned the power of making choices and decisions that resonate with the way I want to feel. How do I want to feel? Radiant, joyful, sovereign, abundant, and connected! I learned how to *be* myself by loving myself and my life without punishing myself for it. I continue to bring my determination and ambition to the table, but now I do it with directed intention and in alignment with my deep, driving desires. And I do it with ease. Now, my accomplishments provide me with infinite joy and meaning rather than hollow and fleeting accolades.

The search for meaning is universally human and the answer is unique to each of us. Although you may not know exactly what you're feeling, why you're feeling it, or where any of this will take you, I want you to know that I honor you as you are. You are exactly where you're meant to be: at the threshold digging your soul out from under your ego.

You are discovering how good it feels to be exactly who you are.

Reflection Questions:

1. *What* is meaningful to you? *Why* is it meaningful? What values, passions, or principles do you relate to or embody at this point in your journey?

____

____

____

____

2. Using one of your defining moments, can you identify an alignment or misalignment of values, ethics, morals, or principles? What did this teach you, and did you integrate the wisdom moving forward?

____

____

____

____

3. Is there an example in your life where you found alignment with someone based on your values? Recall the circumstances and reflect: how did you know you were aligned? How did that feel emotionally and energetically? Compare and contrast that to a time when you entered into an agreement, partnership, or another situation where there was no values alignment with the other person or party. How did *that* feel emotionally and energetically?

____

____

____

____

Actionable Practices:

1. Express your values and principles. Find a time to have a conversation with someone important in your life such as a spouse, partner, colleague, boss, or friend. Talk about your values and inquire into theirs. Start this deep, meaningful conversation. Be open to what comes up, even if it is resistance. What happens in this moment? Notice any changes in the other person and in your understanding of them. Notice how they respond to you.

____

____

____

____

2. Put your most meaningful life on a vision board of some sort. Engage your right brain (imagination, creativity, innovation) to create a visual representation of what brings meaning into your life. Include what you currently have as well as what you desire. Make sure that the vision board is driven by your values and principles. As you build this board, feel into the gratitude and love for all that you already have. Keep your vision board somewhere you can see it every day and connect to it energetically with gratitude and joy!

____

____

____

____

3. Keep your values list in a few accessible places where you can be reminded of them on a daily basis. Whether it's a note on your mirror, a digital reminder, or taped inside the front of your journal, seeing your values will trigger you to align actions, intentions, and relationships to those values.

____

____

____

____

Go Deeper:

Rather than direct you to outside resources or thinkers, I wish to invite you to dive deeper into your own philosophy and framework. What questions have I not asked you? Where do you want to explore further? What are the driving questions or powerful commitments you have established for yourself?

____

____

____

____

This is your opportunity to inquire within. Craft a personal manifesto, draft an open letter, create a list of agreements to live by – whatever it looks like, I want you to ask yourself how you can begin to implement your personal philosophy, meaning, and values framework.

____

____

____

____

CHAPTER 9

Sovereign AF

Mantra:

I am sovereign. I am fearless. I am authentically me.
I am strong in who I am. I honor my truth.
I honor my essence. I express my authenticity.
I expand my sense of Self. I AM.

Keywords:

Expression, Liberation, Creatorship, Individuation,
Expansion, Embodiment

Intuition is a word that describes your ability to harness your multi-dimensional human nature and access your higher self. Through ongoing practice and application of the insights here, you've started to experience the "miraculous" gifts of your intuition. You've aligned more deeply with your inner authority and witnessed firsthand how understanding and accepting your true nature makes you a more powerful leader and creator.

In Chapter 8, you went through a process of self-discovery that cultivated a stronger foundation for the sovereignty that is emerging within you. You established a clear center that keeps you accountable, and now you have anchored into your values and the worth derived from meaning. You are moving with purpose and conviction. You see the connections between intention, attention, and efficacy. You feel the impact you're making and the value you're creating. You are receptive to synchronicity and allow for exponential outcomes. You have started to cultivate and channel grace as a conscious co-creator with your own life.

As we move towards the end of this book, I am reminded again of the process that happens when I hold Circle with others. When we enter that space, we go on a journey together. We begin with our questions, to center ourselves in the self-inquiry that we're about to embark on. We get clear on the ingredients that we are bringing to the table and what our focus will be. As we dive under the surface and start investigating our experience, we usually encounter the challenge, the crisis, or the confusion that brought us here in the first place. We have moments of getting lost and then finding our way back. Each time we come back to our center, we do so with more clarity and acceptance. More aspects of ourselves have been re-integrated along the way. Inevitably, we arrive at the end and to a sense of completion. Although each person has had their unique adventure, there is a shared narrative that connects the dots on a deeper level.

If you recognize yourself in that description, as you have journeyed through this book and the process you've been on, then you are on your way to completing your journey through sacred Circle. This is the power of holding space: witnessing yourself transform in real-time. You have no doubt encountered your own struggles and questions along the way and might be wondering where we will go from here.

I've done my best to share with you the insights and experiences that unlocked my own learnings. I wrote this book to illuminate the teachings and tools that have had the most impact on my own evolution, awakening, and ability to live a fulfilling life. Now that we've covered the core intelligence centers and how they influence our intuition and outlined the framework for discovering our deepest core values, principles, and desires through meaning and alignment, we are going to move into the next chapter of the journey: integration. Anchoring your authority as an expression of sovereignty is important, for that's where you actualize insights through empowered action.

Your authentic nature is the essence of your uniqueness. From traits to funny tics, cultural conditioning to cellular memory, who you are as an individual is meant to be honored – and expressed. The last stage of this journey is embodiment: the total claiming of your power and worth. The full YES of your being.

Here, you get to release into the fullness of who you are. No permission is needed, not even from yourself. At this point, it's pure beingness! There's no more need to play small, for you have felt just how powerful you truly are. This fierce love is a powerful cleansing agent for our old programming and conditioning. It blasts away lingering self-doubt, insecurity, suffocation, and self-sabotage. There are no more excuses left now that you've done the work. You know yourself. You know your responsibility to your divine authority, and you have committed to bringing it forward no matter the cost.

Stop for a second and listen to the anticipation in your body. Breathe it in. This is your essence becoming activated. Your higher self sees the potential waiting to be unleashed and it wants you to leap.

This is a call to awaken you completely. My invitation is this: Step in.

You are ready to move your soul into action. If you are still experiencing any anxiety or fear about the journey ahead, then rest easy knowing this: you are shining the light on what no longer serves you so you can burn away the excess. You are opening the door to a more powerful self and any ideas that don't serve you must be left behind. Release them now if you can.

The work you are doing here is more than self-discovery. It is personal liberation. It is the claiming of your divine birthright. The world needs you ready to serve, and you cannot do that if you are still engaged in self-sabotaging behaviors or self-doubt. You've *always* known what you were capable of and now that knowledge has brought you here.

The world is ready to receive your truest Self yet. The new leadership is authority through authenticity: literally *being* the value. When you recognize your inherent value because you are aligned with it fully, you bring forth more energy, power, and influence into the work at hand. Your impact will be felt by many when you are operating from this space. That doesn't mean the work will be easy. To be in your divine authority is to live outside your ego's comfort zone; to come from the courageous heart of your truth rather than what pleases. This process of alignment will require you to claim yourself fully, to live from your essence; allied to your inner authority. For it is only when you have learned to honor yourself as sovereign that you can accept and honor others as unique sovereign beings. This is the foundation of true respect and equality.

What Makes You, You?

Authenticity is our essence: the honoring of our uniqueness. It represents the agreement made by the collective unconscious to awaken, for it is only when we do the work ourselves that we can help liberate others. Authenticity can be a challenge for some people, as we are trained to think *inside* the box. However, each individual has something to contribute to the awakening of humanity. When we play small and pretend to be who we are not, we are denying the world our greatest gift.

Authenticity and Essence are related. The latter is defined most simply as "the intrinsic nature or indispensable quality of something that determines its character." Each person has their own essence, that which makes you *you*: one-of-a-kind and mathematically impossible to replicate. There is so much room for variation. While every single thing in the known universe is derived from the same base materials, no two combinations are ever alike, and that includes humans.

Is authenticity, as a term, overused? Of course! We talk about this concept all the time as a means of promotion or in service of "speaking our truth," but rarely do we stop to examine and define what authenticity looks like in action. Who are you? What holds value for you? What does your genius look like? What shapes you? How do you identify yourself? The origin of the word identify is Latin and means "to make the same as." So, if you are trying to identify as something or someone outside yourself, then you are not channeling your essence – your gift of being alive. That contribution that only you can make, be it a word, a gesture, or a reflection. You don't have to build an empire, or even a business, to make a meaningful contribution. The only requirement is to show up and allow your essence to shine through. If you're making yourself the same as something else, then how can that be *you*? Being authentic is effortless and easy; it should come naturally, just like breathing.

Deep authenticity is not performative and it's certainly not perfection. It's a working definition of alignment that is constantly evolving and updating itself. It's not a staged, curated life with inspirational captions or catchy tunes. It's not an unfiltered projection or the unwinding of psycho-emotional storylines onto someone else. Authenticity is definitely not speaking your truth in order to hurt another.

Authenticity is the anchoring of awareness into the truth of your heart and coming from that space in your decision-making and action-taking. Authenticity is setting boundaries when something or someone isn't aligned for you. Authenticity is speaking up with compassion. Authenticity is the power to negotiate and compromise, not from obligation, but from your assessment and evaluation of what is right. Authenticity means that even when you get it wrong – and we all do at some point – you are able to sit with this reality, work with it, and integrate the wisdom. Authenticity is accepting all the shadow parts that live within you and recognizing that it's okay to still have work to do. As with everything, your satisfaction and security begin within.

I believe deep authenticity is vital today because the world is awakening at a rapid pace. We can't unsee the things that are coming forward, and we can't bury our heads in the sand at a time when our full awareness is required for both our personal and collective process. We must honor the journey that we are all taking part in, together. When you honor your authenticity and essence, you give others permission to do the same: to step fully into their true Self and live unapologetically from an empowered center. Think of this as igniting a spark. When you are aligned, your energy starts to empower alignment within others. *That's* how easy it can be to lead.

The Guru is You

Turning away from our intuition and following others blindly is why dogma and gurus exist. Authentic expression has always been present for it's an innate part of being human. Yet when we deny and suppress our truth, we project that ability onto others. Influencers are not wiser or better than anyone else, they've just convinced the most people that their voice wins over another's. Yet in a world where rampant disinformation and fake news can circulate the globe in a matter of minutes, we need to cultivate our centers so as not to wobble off course by a well-framed argument.

We've been conditioned to seek this external validation. We have been trained to believe that what others tell us is more valid than our internal metrics and values. Everywhere we go we are told to conform: be this, do this, get this, have that. Make a list of all the things anyone has ever told you to be or do and you will see your basic programming. Humans are wired to minimize risk and reward safety, for that guaranteed our survival for millennia. In the modern world, that ancient evolutionary programming has some interesting side effects.

The pressure to seek external validation is seen most clearly through social media. The compulsive obsession of constantly posting our self-promotion in order to be followed, and follow others. We feel the burden of obligation to always know the answer or do the right thing. We are told not to let our team down, not to make the boss angry, to stay in our lane. We are constantly keeping up with the Jones' in our search to make sense of our world, and our place within it. We feel the burden of obligation because the invisible eyes of our followers hold us hostage to producing more content for the approval of others. We feel obligated to ideas and ideals and "perfect" relationships. But in all this, what truly serves? What is true and authentic? Where do you feel obligated, and why? How might external validation or approval contribute to a feeling of stuckness?

There are many systems dedicated to keeping you disempowered. This isn't a run-of-the-mill conspiracy theory about "the elite" or "dark forces." I'm talking about the whole of what society has been built on, and the violence it has perpetuated against millions of people over hundreds and thousands of years. For those who have been doing the inner work of uncovering bias, racism, sexism, classism, and other embedded systems of segregation and separation within ourselves, we know that these run deep. There are mechanisms to keep the existing system of authority in place. Obedience is a tactic that those in power use to ensure that things stay the same, that no one steps outside the status quo.

Yet this too will be exposed the more people claim their inner authority and step into their sovereignty. When you rule yourself, no one else has the ability to rule over you. We saw the symptoms of this in the #metoo backlash, as women decided that they were no longer going to stay silent about the sexist underbelly of America. And we're seeing the uprising with Black Lives Matter, as people are actively fighting systemic racism, white privilege, and police brutality. We should be actively questioning who wields authority and frugal with how we outsource it. External authority is a privilege to be earned and a responsibility that must be upheld by those who grant it.

Celebrity as authority is another obnoxious idea. It seems that we look to famous people to set the example and show us what to do, rather than do the work ourselves. Take Gwenyth Paltrow, who started her career as an actress, and used her celebrity to launch a business. The influence invested in her by followers granted her the authority to start an online wellness empire. Just because someone is well-known, has status or is in a certain position, or exudes authoritative energy doesn't mean that what they say or what they do should be taken as truth or fact. This is where we practice the discernment that comes from being aligned to our own inner authority. Celebrity influence can be powerful when it helps mobilize for change, but if we are not actively engaged in the work it won't have a significant or lasting effect. No one, no matter how famous or well-intentioned or successful in their own right, knows what is best for you.

Someone else's perfectly curated life is no substitution for our authentic expression. This is a spiritual trap: the idea that you can bypass or skip over the actual work and just enjoy the benefits instead – with a perfectly curated cup of artisanal cacao, posted with the right filter, of course. When you are on the path, there is less time for the performance since you are... actually doing the work! Isn't it funny how many influencers have so much time to curate the perfect social media channel?

When you are committed to being a leader, you know there are more pressing issues at hand that demand your focus and attention. Performing is exhausting. It requires emotional labor. It takes enormous amounts of energy as we are working overtime to sustain the illusion while still dealing with everything else. Being anything but ourselves is depleting in the end – so why do so many of us make that choice again and again? This is a powerful question that we must continue to ask with compassion, and each time we do we peel off another layer, and another, and another.

If you perform to please people, know this: being nice is a myth. It's a self-imposed strangulation of authentic self-expression in order to make someone else feel more comfortable with your truth. Nice is actually *oppressive*. It is politeness that pretends, for it comes with a set of rules about what is acceptable. In other words: it's a form of mind control. I don't like the word nice because I prefer to be real; to express the full range of who I am and what I am capable of feeling, experiencing, and expressing.

Keep in mind that I'm not condoning inappropriate or hateful language, especially after being on the receiving end of trolling and bullying. I value constructive communication and the clarity and resolution that can come from dialogues and respectful arguments. There is a big difference between the oppressive adage "If you have nothing nice to say, don't say anything at all" and expressing displeasure, concern, a boundary, or even anger with self-awareness, civility, and decorum.

As we begin to notice subtle and subversive mechanisms that have caused us to stifle our spirit, and dim our light, we arrive at an inflection point: How much have you been willing to betray yourself for others? This might be an uncomfortable question but it's also a necessary one. This isn't about self-judgment but rather developing that awareness rooted in total love and acceptance. Receive your answers with compassion and make a conscious decision to shift what doesn't feel in alignment. If you find yourself angry at this self-violation, don't turn it against yourself or onto others. Instead, channel it into action and a commitment to never go back to this place of violence again. Grief, anger, resentment, despair, and guilt are all indications that you have violated your values or allowed someone else to violate your boundaries. Pay attention and listen if they come up at any point, for they have something powerful to share with you. This is how you begin the process of atonement and reconciliation necessary for you to live authentically.

Rebooting Your Inner Authority

The only power struggle you've ever had is with yourself. This is the hard reboot moment when you acknowledge that you are the one ultimately responsible for everything in your world. You have been undergoing a rapid evolutionary process of re-examining your relationship with authority and transmuting your pre-existing attachments and structures that were previously built upon limiting beliefs.

You are now ending THE struggle. The one that has divided you your entire life. The one that has forced you to wrestle with your ego and your soul, your small self and your true Self, your external influencers, and your internal authority. You are being called to take ownership of your destiny, to rise up, and take a stand for what you are here to do and be. When you are empowered, you are truly free, for nothing limits your reach. When you feel small, helpless, disempowered, or unworthy, you give your power away to things outside of you. This is when we need to be most vigilant of ourselves because it is in these moments that we are tempted to be rescued by someone else.

The world changed almost overnight in just the first half of the new decade of the 2020s. There is a significant and tangible shift in the ways human beings are relating to one another. Separated by distance and exposed in our structural inequities, we are being asked to become more self-aware and conscious of how we interact. This new world is requiring everyone to have more emotional integrity, to do the deep internal work to uncover implicit bias and internalized racism, to communicate in nonviolent and loving ways. We can no longer be asleep to the corruption inherent in a system that is designed to disempower, disengage, and dehumanize by telling us that authority belongs to those in power and authenticity is unacceptable.

Authenticity and authority can only be exercised through choice. When you choose yourself, you are not choosing yourself over another. This is a false binary that has kept us stuck for far too long; perpetuating cycles of shame and psychological entrapment. You can choose how you want to respond to and show up for life's challenges and unexpected moments. Every day presents us with multiple moments to shift our perspective and evolve ourselves. Are you meeting life with all you have? Or are you sliding back into the victim mindset and waiting for someone else to take action? The choice, of course, is always yours.

No one signs up for the shit. I didn't ask to be bullied as a kid by my classmates and 4th-grade teacher. I didn't choose to suddenly lose my hearing. I didn't want Barrington to die early of cancer. I didn't say yes to being stalked, to being cheated on, to being defrauded, to being trolled. Believe me, I didn't make those choices willingly. True, I have made choices that created less than desirable outcomes, but sometimes life just hands you interesting challenges. Moments are neutral. Now I ask myself: How do I choose to be, given this situation? Do I sit in my ugly feelings forever or do I let them go? Do I identify with the negative or the positive? How will I respond?

Our will creates the momentum necessary to sustain our choices. When we use our willpower to direct our energy, we intend for something to happen. This is not the same willpower that infomercials have co-opted to sell more exercise equipment. This is big, intentional energy that makes your desires manifest. Will is defined as "energetic determination:" no doubts and no hesitation. Declaring your intent to the world can have miraculous consequences, for you have already decided that it will be done. Now the universe simply has to rearrange itself, for you have promised to meet it halfway. If you truly intend for something to happen, you will manifest the energy, tools, and resources to make it so. That is the power of this empowered action word. Notice how many times in your day you say you *will* do something. Observe: how many times do you truly intend to follow through? What would happen if you knew that everything you committed to would happen since your word is your bond?

Now, how many times do you say you "should" or "ought" to do something? Do you notice the difference? Willing yourself to do something is a commandment, a sacred agreement, a contract. A should is a guilt trip, an admonishment. Saying "I ought to" is a sign of obligation to something other than yourself. If you are true to yourself, then there is no question of what you want to do. It's clear where you are aligned and what is a yes, what is a no, and where you need more information to make a clear decision.

Fate and Free Will

Your fate is influenced by your actions. It's easy to think that when something goes wrong that you have made an error from which there is no turning back. This can lead to feeling out of control or unable to face the challenges that come up from time to time. Fate is an escape hatch, a way of distracting ourselves with the idea that we don't have a say in what transpires in our lives, or that someone else is better suited to solving our problems than we are. Yet everything we've encountered along the way can serve us moving forward if we know how to integrate the lesson inside. Every person and situation has an inherent place and purpose on our evolutionary journey.

I now understand that many of the patterns, habits, behaviors, and conditioning that ruled me for most of my life compelled certain responses and reactions. Now I trust my path and my unfolding destiny. I trust myself, so I am more able to relax in the face of this thing we call fate. I know that I alone influence the trajectory of my future and that my response will determine how good or bad things feel throughout the process. As my level of consciousness increases, I am more empowered to shape my life as a co-creator with these forces. I no longer get mad (for too long) if something unexpected temporarily blocks my path, for I know that I'm not a victim of circumstance.

Instead of seeing the old stories inside specific situations, I now see the interplay of mystical teachings and spiritual truths. Now, I have conversations with the lessons as if they were a living, breathing teacher. They are certainly mirrors for my growth. The hard moments I've had along the way were part of the unique recipe for my soul's development. By encountering these challenges, I had the opportunity to develop weaker parts and refine strong ones. I got to see more of myself rise to the situation. And I got to finally experience my full power and sovereignty.

Are you powerless? Absolutely not. Can you control your surroundings? Not really. So, within fate, there is free will. That power comes from choosing your response in every situation, no matter how minor or massive. As Holocaust survivor, psychiatrist and author Victor Frankl said: "In our response lies our growth and freedom."

In 2019 I met Brenda Tracy at a Women of Strength event where we were both speakers. Her story, which she shared on stage, was incredibly painful and also very impactful, if only because she had managed to turn her deep trauma into potent lessons and truths for the audience. Brenda had been gang-raped by a group of college athletes when she was in college, and the institution had done its best to cover up the incident. Until Brenda fought back. She wasn't seeking revenge; she was committed to making real change happen. For years now she's been touring campuses, speaking to athletes, and telling her story; changing lives through the power of her personal transformation. Her truth no doubt makes some uncomfortable. I imagine sharing that story, again and again, might get hard at times but that doesn't stop Brenda. She's changed legislation, opened up important dialogues, and advocated for victims who don't have a voice. By being herself fully and inviting us into her story, we get to experience the power of her message.

When we engage life like this, we pivot into self-mastery. The self-important or superficial facades start to drop away as we take our power back. Power is an agent of change, and if we are unwilling to be that for ourselves, we become disempowered. One prerequisite for self-mastery is a type of emotional maturity. The less you blame others around you for your problems, the more you are stepping into taking responsibility for your emotions and needs. True sovereignty is total responsibility.

It's time to ditch the guru if you haven't already. The real wisdom lives within you, and now you must claim yourself in order to start the next chapter and move forward on the path. If you haven't connected the dots by now, then let it be known: *you* are the inner authority you are cultivating, and the best thing you can do for your evolution is learn to identify, align with, and trust this space within. It is your true source of power, and it's available to you at any moment.

Our reality is a reflection of all that we believe is possible, and we contain every possibility within ourselves. From this perspective, our only challenge is to cultivate a mindset that recognizes this truth so we can more fully inhabit it. Each issue or problem that comes your way is resolving itself in your mind first. When it's no longer viewed as an issue internally, it will cease to become one that stands in your way.

Leading With Authenticity

The leadership needed in our world today is authority through authenticity: leading through being. The old command and control ways are over. We are replacing these outdated approaches with the willingness to learn and grow through our mistakes; our ability to be vulnerable and open, to show the way forward through our willingness to walk it with grace and humility. This is how we guide each other through the portal of awakening.

Are you brave enough to ask yourself: "What if I'm wrong about this?" If you are willing to confront your sacred ego, you are on the path. You can only lead others as far as you are willing to lead yourself. Your ability to diffuse, integrate, and share your most powerful learnings and toughest challenges is a function of your commitment to authentic leadership. Real leaders are "all for all" and do their best to empower their team to step into their own sovereignty and inner authority. Collective success happens when people are allowed to find freedom inside their individual choices, expression, and alignment.

True leaders show up with their humanity. They show up without performing or pretending because they are established and centered in their trust of themselves. Command and control, top-down, hierarchical, prove-it-to-me leadership styles are not effective, for they don't gain the respect they are attempting to extract. "Leaders" who engage in power plays or subversive manipulation tactics are not embodied in their power, hence their desire to control everyone around them.

True leaders are people we can invest our trust in, especially in a time of crisis. Leaders who demonstrate empathy, compassion, and courage gain our respect, for we want our leaders to remain present with the needs of those they serve. Good leaders have clear boundaries and know how to communicate them effectively, for they are usually trying to motivate others around a meaningful cause or effort.

A true leader is actually leading themselves first. The rest of us follow because the example they set is honorable and commands respect. From that perspective, the authority we are cultivating is over our own lives, not over anyone else. This authority can only be cultivated by connecting to the experiences that have shaped us along the way. It emerges from self-reflection and self-inquiry, inner work, and awareness; through time spent facing the shadows and ugly feelings we don't like and still showing up regardless. Leadership emerges from the ability to honor ourselves - every single facet and dimension. If we are doing an exceptionally good job at this, others will usually follow – because they are inspired.

The Inner Divine Authority

As you can see, the old definition and paradigm of authority is something or someone outside of ourselves, based on a hierarchical system seeking to maintain itself. Now our world is experiencing a reckoning and the system as we knew it is in a state of entropy. What is rising up to stand in its place? Authenticity: heart-centered, aware, compassionate leadership of the self.

We live in a world now where more people recognize that systems of hierarchy and policing don't work for them. They don't want to be told what to do or who to be. They want to understand themselves and the world, and they are willing to learn and grow along the way. With your developed awareness and connection to your intuitive powerhouse, you will be better able to discern those who are manipulating and driven by self-interest and those who are aware, in their integrity, and attuned to their center. The more you cultivate your inner authority and move into actions that reflect its expression, the more you will realize that being in power means being of service.

We no longer ask, "Why is this happening to me?" Rather, we reflect on "Why is this happening for me?" We don't assume that something went wrong because it ended. We trust that what is meant to be, and will be. We witness ourselves lead without force and create impact with loving actions. We change all stereotypes by not assuming they are finite structures, but rather systems of belief that may or may not be in service to our growth. We stop acting the way we are expected to and start being who we really are.

Direct Your Authority Through Choice

Our ability to choose is one of our greatest powers in action. No matter what life presents us with, we always have the opportunity to choose our response. In moments of particular struggle or hardship, we can ask ourselves what limiting patterns are in play, whether we agree with them or want to update them. Then we act accordingly. We can stay in limiting mindsets or elevate ourselves through the power of choice at any time.

The more you choose to show up for yourself, the more you will be given opportunities to do your deepest healing. Your breakdown *is* the breakthrough if you choose to believe it. Harnessing the mind helps you use this powerful tool to serve your evolution, not keep you stuck in "Old You." So use it. Let the left brain tear down every faulty fantasy and assumption that tells you what you can't do and ask your right brain to fuel you with bold new ideas.

It's precisely in those moments when life isn't going to plan that we want to throw our hands up and let someone else figure it out. Yet these are the moments when we are being asked to show up fully and respond from a more empowered perspective. These are the moments when we call upon our intuition, transcendent intelligence centers, and heart. It will take time to cultivate trust and faith in your process, especially as you're developing your intuition.

Your transformation isn't a one-time event that can be penciled in at your convenience. It demands your authentic participation, your humility, and your patience. If you are committed to deep change, know that your evolution will test everything you knew to be true. You will stop pleasing people and making yourself small. Your human transformation will be honest, raw, hopeful, ugly, beautiful, and ultimately divine. You will shift how you see the world because the world is changing to respond to you. And *that* is part of the work you are here to do.

Claim What's Already Yours

Divine authority holds the key to your greatest reinvention, reconfiguration of purpose, and the redefinition of your personal agreements, commitments, boundaries, and foundational structures. This is the moment of truth. Today is a defining moment that can alter the framework of your entire reality, restoring your power and authority – if you choose that to be true for you.

You are the only authority in your life. By now I hope you see that no outside entity or external institution can be responsible for your liberation. You must be the one to choose to live authentically and free yourself from any enslavement systems or constructs. What could you accomplish or create when you step into your full power? What could you accomplish or achieve if you trusted yourself fully? When you decide to commit fully, the universe will be right there to meet you.

To claim something implies total alignment, commitment, and responsibility – regardless of the outcome. If you haven't done so yet, it's time to claim yourself fully: your voice, your body, your emotions, your mind, your wisdom, your heart, your experience, your truth. Claim your sovereignty. Claim your authority. Claim your authentic essence. Why? Because claiming is an act of empowerment.

In doing this, you are acknowledging, accepting, honoring, and integrating all that was you and making it available to who you are now. By making a claim, you are alchemizing, digesting, processing, composting, and transmuting the elements of your life (people, experiences, situations, challenges, successes, and trauma) and shifting them into a higher perspective. All those things served your growth in the end. They should be recognized for where they have led you on the path.

Deep authenticity gives you the inner strength that radiates out in everything: from thought to action to manifestation. It's a form of inner strength that allows us to push past the discomfort that holds us back from claiming our sovereign life. When you honor your essence, authenticity, and the divine authority in yourself, you do the same for others.

We're smashing the paradigm of sameness. This unspoken program states that in order to be liked or accepted by others we have to be more like them, thus shutting down and ignoring our most powerful gifts. For centuries, humans have sought to be similar, to minimize risk, because that is what kept us safe and accepted; able to participate in social structures. Yet the same agreements that bonded us and created order also served to divide; promoting separation, power struggles, destruction, and needless death. One of my favorite and most profound quotes is from Maharishi Mahesh Yogi: "Unity is thy nature, Diversity is thy glory."

An important distinction: *sameness* is not unity. *Sameness* is identifying with a set of parameters determined by others as acceptable or agreeable. No one is alike, although we can find similar points of reference and relate to one another. Although we are not the same, we can still be unified in our service of each other and the Earth.

The New Paradigm of Productivity

We are united in our uniqueness and our beautiful imperfections. It's time to do away with the false ideal of perfection. Attempting to be overly perfectionist is counter-productive. Allow perfection to be a continual process of aspiration, a rich journey of living into your deep, driving desires.

One of the most challenging lessons to learn is that of accepting everything as is, for all is perfect. Do you feel the judgment rise within you as you hear this? What about righteousness? Or disbelief? The complete rejection of such an *absurd* notion. The evil, the pain, the suffering, the hatred – how can that be perfect?! I don't claim to have answers for you. I sit with these inquiries sometimes and I still find it hard to accept, especially if I'm trying to do so with my linear mind.

This is simply our humanness. I have had deeply transcendent moments, where I have *known* this as truth. I have experienced the perfection of life. I have known deep bliss and perfection within, as I looked out at the world through these eyes. Then I got up and made dinner. I carried on with the everyday and honored the mundane. When we look out at the world through eyes of judgment, we will always find something wrong. When we look out at the world through the eyes of the heart, we will always find the beauty, the love, and the perfection waiting to greet us.

In acceptance of that which we cannot change, we refocus on that which we *can* change. Instead of outer perfection, what if we were focused on perfecting our attention, intention, and actions? The actualization of creative potential is at the heart of our nature. What are you producing in life? With your thoughts, emotions, words, and deeds – and do those satisfy you deeply?

Mindfulness is perfection in action. Strive to approach all endeavors with mindfulness, integrity, awareness, and heart-centered, intentional action. Give yourself the space to check external information against your inner knowing and don't take everything at face value just because someone has authority on the issue. Ask yourself, "Does this feel right in my gut? Is it aligned to my values and meaning? Does it advance my deep, driving desires?" You can do this for all future decisions, choice points, and forks in the path ahead. That's how you give yourself the space and permission to be imperfect, to try, to fail, and to learn.

We can't be productive when we are burnt out. We can't be productive when we're overwhelmed by emotions. We can't be productive when we're ruminating on the past or trying to make predictions of the future; nor when the mind is running rampant. We can't be productive when we are overcome by grief or rage, or when we're exhausted or sick. We can't be productive when we're dissonant or out of alignment. We can't be productive when rooted in patterns, habits, and beliefs rooted in scarcity, lack, and limitation. We can't be productive when we aren't honoring our sovereignty; we can't be productive if we don't honor others.

Intuition is productive. So, go with your inspiration, go with your enthusiasm, go with your gut, go with your desires, and go with your heart.

Reflection Questions:

1. In what situations do I most easily give my power away? Why?

____

____

____

____

2. In what areas of life have I woken up to my power?

____

____

____

____

3. To whom am I an authority? To whom am I a leader? How do I lead them? Am I leading myself with honor?

____

____

____

____

Actionable Practices:

1. List all the situations in your life right now that make you feel powerless, obstructed, denied, or suppressed. As you review them, ask yourself: Can you shift these perceived limitations by seeing them differently? Is there a choice you can make about any of these things so that they don't feel negative? Are there actions you can take to change the outcomes if any of these are constant or recurring?

____

____

____

____

2. Claim what you are calling into your life now. To claim something implies personal responsibility, choice, and action all at the same time. You can do this by declaring:

   "I claim _________________."

____

____

____

____

3. List all the qualities about yourself that you love, or would love to have. Don't be shy. Go crazy and tap into the ones that feel the best, and the easiest to embody. Review them, and as you do so, see where

you can spot any opportunities to bring those qualities forward more often. Make a commitment to change your habitual reactions or patterns in order to let these qualities shine.

Go Deeper:

In addition to astrology, numerology, and energetic divination tools, these are others for discovering our soul's blueprint and also some business-related ones that tell us about our traits and qualities:

- Human Design

- Enneagram

- Gene Keys

- Fascination Advantage Test

- Myers Briggs Test

CHAPTER 10:

Full Circle

Mantra:

I am connected. I am important.

I am supported by my community.

I am supported by Mother Earth.

I am an important part of the greater whole.

Keywords:

Cycles, Spirals, Community, Connection,

Natural, Kinship, Humanity

We are now entering the final cycle of our journey together. From here forward, you will be stepping into an expanded center and putting your intuition and wisdom practices into action. If you are dedicated and determined to see real growth, you will continue learning how to hold yourself accountable within the interconnected web of your community and in doing so, witness the deep impact of the work you've done here.

This book can only take you so far. What I have shared with you is invaluable – but only if you decide to commit to the integration process fully. You are not alone in this journey. As an individual, you are responsible for the inner work, but when it comes to true healing, we must do this in relation to one another. The real practice is applying the learnings in relationships, for it is in the crucible of relationship that we are able to see who we are and what we are not.

Life is the real teacher. We will be given every opportunity to learn the lessons that matter. More often than not, we encounter those teachings through people. We have come full circle when we master the concept through practice. When faced with the same challenge, you now choose a different response; one that is aligned with your awakened inner authority.

Keep in mind that the mind doesn't always feel ready. Transformation is rarely linear; more often than not we are expanding on multiple fronts at once. You might feel effective in certain areas of your life and disempowered in others. That doesn't mean you haven't grown. Rather, it's important to remember that in coming home to your sovereign self, you are aligning to a different kind of rhythm; one that isn't dictated by others' terms, outcomes, or motivations. You are on your own schedule. Inner work rarely follows a linear path. Your process is its own cycle, and you will most likely repeat it a few times before you have fully mastered each practice.

This is an invitation to drop fully into the spiraling nature of your evolution and witness yourself. This chapter is about building and strengthening your center so that as you step into the flow of life with more tools, you feel capable of navigating the cycles that will naturally arise. This is the final attunement process and one that is designed to support you in bringing all you have learned to life.

Closing the Circle

When you began this book, you were standing at the threshold of a portal. You didn't know yet what existed on the other side – but you trusted the transformation ahead. Now, you are changed. Whether you feel it or not, you have upgraded your internal programming and stepped into a new cycle. A single action, done differently after a lifetime of the same response, alters your course forever. This is power that you've unleashed in opening this book: something unlocks and you find a key to a door you weren't sure you would ever open.

This is a book that is fundamentally about YOU. You've spent a lot of time in this realm as you connected to your inner authority, authentic essence, and deep driving desires. You've been on a journey of deep inner work that has allowed you greater access to your innate, embodied wisdom. You have seen firsthand what you are capable of and you've no doubt had opportunities to practice along the way. For some of you, it might be the most time you've ever committed to yourself. The more you embody the concepts you've learned here, the more powerful you become. Thus it's imperative to get to know yourself better than anyone else.

That's why taking the work out into the world is mission-critical: because everything is connected. Even things that feel millions of miles away. You live within a home, which occupies space in a city, which is located somewhere on a continent inhabiting planet Earth. But it doesn't stop there – the earth is an ecosystem that exists inside of a solar system; itself part of a galaxy. Systems live inside systems, and this pattern goes on forever. Nothing is isolated, regardless of whether the story we tell about our experience says otherwise. Understanding this is essential: your evolution depends on everything else.

The reverse is true too: everything else depends on you, too. That's why doing the inner work brings such immense benefits: not only does it serve your growth, but everyone else grows alongside you. Certainly, it doesn't always feel that way, but that's how life works. It's not as complex as it sounds, for nature is organized on a simple foundational principle: from a quantum molecule to the holographic universe, everything starts as a circle. The cell, one of the building blocks of life, is a circle. And as this circle expands, it takes on new shapes, but it never loses touch with its original essence. The cell has rhythms that advance its own evolution, and it works within these cycles to achieve a critical momentum in order to fuel *growth*.

Change is another fundamental organizing principle. In order to grow, things must change. Resisting this process will create suffering, for it runs counter-intuitive to life itself. As we change, we evolve – and yet we encounter similar learnings and lessons at each stage of life. This is why I like to think of myself as a circle, and my process as a cycle.

The Symbolism of Circles

The shape of the circle is a symbol that has been used since the beginning of time. It is an archetypal form, in that multiple cultures and peoples have recognized its significance throughout history. Often representing the "'whole," the circle is a symbol of completion, of recognizing that which was always true and thus is eternal in nature.

Circles are associated with cycles, which operate slightly differently. A cycle indicates that we will pass through familiar stages in the same way that each year has four seasons, although how we will spend each season depends on who we are at that moment. A cycle is not about getting stuck in a way of doing things – hence the term "run in circles" – but rather appreciating that each stage has its gifts and its lessons. A cycle will allow you to revisit old stories and beliefs each time you encounter a familiar trigger or challenge, but it will never return you to a previous state of being.

Circles reconnect us with the organic rhythms that run the universe. They are potent reminders of the fact that there are no straight lines in nature. Thinking of ourselves as walking a linear path can be counterintuitive, for this idea takes us away from something, forgetting the point of origin as we get further ahead on the path. What actually happens is that we spiral around our lessons and learn different facets of ourselves through our ongoing engagement with our perceived challenges and constructed storylines. In a cyclic rhythm, one is always connected to the thread of life inside. When we are connected to the natural cycles of life, we don't forget our lessons or leave them behind. Instead, we build upon them because we can always see it and return to it if we forget something important we learned. And inevitably, we will!

The circle is a reflection of life itself. Many cultures have used the symbol of the circle in their spiritual practices and traditions. From this perspective, the origin is always in sight and we move around it, regarding it with new eyes as we evolve. The circle contains both the beginning and the end, it is a companion that guides us and not something to be left behind. Keep that in mind next time you are tempted to judge your process because you believe you've taken two steps back.

No wonder we adorn royals with a circular crown! This symbol is potent with potential. Now that you are claiming your sovereignty, consider this chapter your final initiation.

The Creative Power of Natural Cycles

From the perspective of the circle, everything is a mirror. When we look at what is opposite of us – or what we oppose – we might be surprised by the reflection we find. This is the power of returning to the beginning: to see how far we've come in our response to the familiar. If we reject something, we don't give ourselves the opportunity to learn from the challenge it presents us.

The greatest teacher is nature, and nature runs on cycles. Just because you encounter one thunderstorm and survive doesn't mean you'll be free of rain forever. Weather patterns move around the world, the moon revolves around the Earth, which in turn revolves around the Sun. Many creatures migrate in cyclic patterns, roaming far yet returning each year to raise their young again. Plants sprout, bloom, produce fruit, and drop seeds to ensure their continued renewal the next season.

Cycles abound in every dimension and humans have used them throughout history to live in harmony with the Earth. Yet somewhere along the line, humans stopped trying to replicate and learn from nature's evolutionary mechanisms; deviating from the original relationship to exert further power and influence. We went from symbiosis to subjugation in a few hundred years or less, completely upending the inherent cycles that govern everything. The lesson humanity as a whole is still learning is how to work within these deeply interwoven and intricate systems so as to live synergistically – that is, in relationship to the larger whole that contains us.

The idea of a container is inherent when we visualize a circle. We see a complete unit and feel a relaxed centeredness when we contemplate a circle. It is the same idea with our sovereignty: the sovereign self is contained but not closed, centered but not controlling. It is an organic, innate state of being that has always existed and won't leave, for it is already complete. There is nothing further to seek here; only the divine authority to remember and relax into.

In the same way that this book is a container to hold you through your transformation, your sovereignty is the container that holds you through life. By attuning to your own cycles, you start to work with, rather than resist, the movement or change that naturally wants to occur. This is because evolution is organic! It will happen whether we want it to or not, yet if we choose to work *with* the cycle we will go farther in the long run.

Sometimes it feels like we spend all of our time doing the inner work. When we ask ourselves "Why does it feel so hard?" it's because we're not in alignment with the flow of intuition and natural rhythms. When we force, we are actually working against ourselves. It usually emerges when we take a linear, hard-nosed approach with our self-development. Believing that if we just do X, we will receive Y. I know this tendency very well because I spent the first part of my journey trying to "break through". I approached my awakening the same way I got through the hardest moments in my journey: by pushing harder. The irony is that what really accelerated my integration were the things I resisted most of all: surrender and rest.

Many of us are making the transformational journey harder on ourselves because we have bought into the linear belief that working hard equals success. The idea of ease and flow is conflated with laziness or luck, rather than what it is: alignment.

When you attune to natural cycles, you disrupt linear patterns. Consider: how connected are you to the core rhythms of the natural world? Do you rise with the sun and go to sleep when it sets? Do you appreciate the waning and waxing of the moon? Do you celebrate the end of things just as much as the beginning? Nothing starts and stops, it always emerges from something else – another connection, another relationship, another step. The more you pay attention to the rhythms and cycles that surround you, the more you will become aware of the inevitability of change.

Holding Circle

The story of Circle began long before my awakening. I was attending a yoga retreat in Ecuador in 2013 when I met a yoga teacher named Ashley Turner, who planted an important seed. I was in the process of coming back to myself as a woman and learning about natural cycles and how they impacted me. Right around this time, Ashley used the word Priestess in reference to herself – and she was. It was as though I was remembering a long-forgotten part of myself, for in just hearing the word I came alive.

Ashley shared with me about a project she wanted to bring to life: a program for women to learn the ancient teachings from "lost" underground cultures. It called forth images of women who had been burned at the stake hundreds of years ago for sharing similar ideas. In those days, a woman could be tortured and killed just for walking alone in the woods or for using herbs to heal an illness or wound. Men in power feared the primal connection to nature that many women (and even some men) enjoyed. Perhaps they sensed that our attunement to natural cycles made us more powerful and decided to punish this connection. Consider the spiritual dimension of this power struggle: in privileging intellect over intuition as a "knowing," they turned people's true natures against them. Suddenly, external authority took over and inner authority was minimized.

Yet now we return once again to the beginning of a great cycle. I sat in my first circle in September 2013 when Ashley, along with her collaborator and another ordained priestess, Sianna Sherman, held one of their first Urban Priestess gatherings in Venice Beach. It was unlike anything I'd ever attended. It wasn't the yoga class I was used to; it was a deep inner practice that was shared in communion with other women. I had never felt so feminine as I did that weekend.

Two years later, Ashley and Sianna launched the full Urban Priestess mystery school. This program was designed to reconnect women with their true feminine nature based on the cycles of life. It took all the linear frameworks I had been working with up until that point and flipped them on their head.

Instead of a calendar full of squares, we followed the Wheel of the Year. This was the same natural calendar that most ancient cultures followed until Pope Gregory introduced his version in the 1500s. Unfortunately, the Gregorian calendar was not an improvement, although it superseded all others – mostly as a result of being forced upon the dominant culture and indigenous "conquered" peoples. The Wheel of the Year is mathematically perfect, for it is based on the natural cycles of the Earth, sun, and the moon. There is no mechanistic time-keeping here. This is pure synchronization.

We absorbed teachings from ancient cultures all around the world: mythology and mysticism, diverse spiritual practices, and religious traditions. We learned how to make intentional changes in our lives in accordance with the natural cycles. It was here that I saw how such simple changes defied logic, for they weren't organized in a linear fashion. I experienced how much courage it took to go against society's rules, especially those that had effectively vilified and silenced women and indigenous cultures.

As I connected more deeply to my rhythms, my life changed. I could more easily identify when something in my world felt "off" or was not in alignment. I started to feel what "right" in my body felt like and what didn't support me. I learned to work with my body rather than against it. The impact of this simple yet profound teaching on cycles was obvious: after nearly 11 years of perimenopause that began when I was 24, I had my first natural period.

Urban Priestess is no longer operational, yet the teachings live on within me. What I learned here was the power of the ritual within my practices: I cultivated a sovereign connection to myself that was rooted in a rhythm; a cycle. Fundamentally, it demonstrated the power of embodying the work we do in the world. Not just mindlessly performing tasks, but moving through the rhythm of life with a conscious awareness, an aligned essence, and a fearless inner authority.

The Biology of Life

There are a few basic categories of natural cycles that deserve deeper examination. You might be familiar with some of these already. If that's the case for you, I invite you to bring your new level of awareness to this examination, as you might see your rhythms differently now that you've shifted inside.

Many of us are aware of cycles, but how many of you use them consciously? Let's start with the body and the physical self, as this is one of the easiest ways to ground the understanding of cycles. Everything begins here. *Chronobiology* is a term that refers to a field of study that examines periodic or cyclic phenomena in living organisms and how that relates to their adaptation. Science is showing us how to honor these rhythms as well as the variations within, for each of us have our own unique adaptations.

The human body is masterful and is able to sustain multiple rhythms at once. Your breath cycle is one such rhythm, your circadian cycle is another. These rhythms regulate natural changes in your body's chemicals and functionality, acting as a master clock that coordinates the other mechanisms in your body. When your body is dysregulated in one of your biological rhythms, you feel the difference.

The four biological rhythms are circadian, ultradian, diurnal, and infradian. Of these, the circadian rhythm is the most well known to us, but all of them help govern and regulate appetite, sleep, hormones, body temperature, energy, performance – and so much more. Women are naturally more attuned to cycles and tend to feel their fluctuation more so than men.

Yet, we are also more prone to feeling disconnected from these cycles – take, for instance, menstruation, the fifth biological cycle exclusive to a woman's body. While many women were taught to feel shame about their period, learning how to honor and work with this rhythm can actually create more alignment than trying to hide its presence. Getting into sync and tracking these changes along with how it impacts mood, emotions, and energy levels is important and increases subtle awareness about our body state.

Whether you are a woman or a man, when you know the rhythms of your body, you also know the right times to undertake different activities with more success: creative tasks, focused work, strength or endurance activities, rest, recuperation, play, or romance, etc.

Humanity used to live in attunement with nature – that is, until modern agricultural practices allowed for constant production of food regardless of the season or temperature outside. Humans stopped working within the traditional natural framework and started modifying the process, making it more artificial and monolithic as we went along. Now we've been denatured by the primacy of intellect and industrialization and our bodies and planet are struggling to keep up with the mess we've created. The disconnect from the core rhythms of life itself has made our relationship with our sacred home – Mother Earth, a challenging, contentious one.

Intuitively, we know that nature is good for us. Nature has always been a part of our human world and, more correctly, humans have always been part of the natural world, and our bodies know how to adjust accordingly. Consider how your appetite and activities change when it's the winter versus the summer. Think of how your body feels in each opposing season. The seasons allow us to enjoy different phases of life that are completely natural and allow for a full process to unfold. It's clear we shouldn't rush this or try and shortcut it in any way, and yet we have; creating results less than desirable over the long term.

There are many documented physical, emotional, and mental health benefits to being outside in nature. You don't need to go camping or even leave your yard to enjoy the healing opportunities that nature provides. For instance, you can practice Earthing: a simple practice of putting your bare feet on the ground. Letting your skin connect with grass and soil is essential to feeling connected, grounded, and revived, for the exchange of ions between your body and the Earth is beneficial to your immune and nervous systems. One thing has been made clear by decades of research: nature is good for your health, and probably in more ways than we can even currently imagine.

If you live in an urban setting and don't have access to green spaces, consider how you might bring more plants *into* the home! Cultivating plants and bringing flowers into the home can help improve your mood even if you don't have a park or green space nearby. Regardless of where you are, you can always enjoy a beautiful sunset from your window; turn off your air conditioning and feel the heat of the air outside, or take yourself on a hike during the weekend. No matter how minute, these simple moments can serve to reconnect you to that sense every human feels when in nature – to *something* bigger than yourself.

Connecting to the Lunar Rhythm

At this point, the question we want to answer is: how can we effectively center our consciousness in the natural movement and flow of life, thereby cultivating more harmony, greater connection, and alignment of outcomes?

My own process has shown me that conscious participation with the lunar rhythms has brought me greater ease, purpose, and clarity in my foundational practice of attunement and alignment. I can more easily welcome my daily experience within the context of this natural rhythm, and it has since become a cornerstone of my inner cycles. When we get into coherence with life, we learn to work with it and not against it. That's how cycles support us. We feel less thwarted by the outcome when we understand where we are in the rhythm of it all.

Each moon phase provides us with a different energetic tone and has qualities that we can tune into in order to be more supported in our lives. Generally, the New Moon is a time of beginnings: a time to get quiet and listen, to go within and notice the subtle cues and synchronicities that might be signaling to you. It is a great moment to intentionally plant new ideas, intentions, or seeds for the future you desire. Energetically, it can feel quiet; like the dark before the dawn.

The Full Moon, on the other hand, is a time of culmination and harvest, a time of ripening. It's a good time to see what is bearing fruit in your life and whether you need to trim any thorny bushes back. It's a great time to let go of anything that isn't serving you or to push out into the world the ideas and energy that is most exciting, inspiring, and alive to you. The Full Moon holds a lot of manifestation energy, so it's a powerful time to work with your natural rhythms.

Each new moon offers subtle transformation if we are aware enough to notice it. You will notice how the cycle includes several phases: the first stirrings, the slow awakening of growth, then the excited upswing, and finally a culmination of some sort. You take the energy in and transform it through your experience, riding the wave alongside the cycle, so to speak. When it's complete, you release it with the next cycle of the moon taking root.

For women, this is an essential attunement practice. We have, on average, 13 menstrual cycles of 28 days, which correspond to the natural lunar cycles each year. I have found that getting deeper into lunar attunement has helped me better accept my emotions and support my energy levels while seeing myself with more compassion and grace. It's also given me the tools to better communicate what's happening in my world and what I need.

You can't collect the water when it's not raining. You can't harvest plants when they're seedlings and expect mature fruit. Humans are no different! We must cultivate, resource, and gestate before we can bloom and bear fruit. Living in a more rhythmic way allows us to better tap into and access our transcendent intelligence. You'll feel and be more receptive to what comes your way, and you'll be able to tune into your intuition more clearly.

Circle of Sovereignty

Before holding Circle, I thought I was the only one who had the following issues: denial, disliking discomfort and not wanting to face uncomfortable conversations, worrying too much about what others think, worrying that I was "too much," worrying I wasn't good enough, fears of rejection, humiliation, and being misunderstood, trying to do the right thing by others but secretly feeling resentful, not knowing how to assert my power effectively, not asking for help, being independent to a fault, and pining for things that weren't good for me – and this is the shortlist!

I'm guessing many of you have struggled with some or all of these and most likely other challenges that I didn't list. Have you felt alone in your struggle? Do you feel that you couldn't express a doubt or fear to others because you might be judged, rejected, ostracized, humiliated, exiled, abandoned, wounded, or hurt somehow? What if I told you that no matter what your worst feeling or thought is, someone is willing to listen and hold space for it without judgment? How would you feel then? Would you be tempted to let someone in and meet you there?

When I decided to offer my first Circle as a facilitator, I felt the strongest yes in my heart. I felt joy and determination that I hadn't felt in a very long time. I was one year into the dark night of the soul and my constant state of confusion and frustration was not serving me. For many months, I hadn't experienced any clarity or direction. So when this idea to hold a Circle came through with so much force and feeling, I moved quickly. I sent out invitations and received a lot of positive responses. I mapped out every detail of the evening over the course of a week, and on the day of Circle I cleaned, cooked, shopped for supplies, and set up the house. With great care, I set up the altar space and went over the ten pages of notes I had prepared. I was nervous yet deeply inspired.

A few hours before I started getting the texts: "I can't make it…", "Sorry, I need to do other things…" With each text, my heart sank and my joy turned into doubt. My mind was full of the inner critic's shrill cries of "I told you this was a bad idea!" I started to review all my possible missteps along the way. There were plenty of other soundbaths and wellness events that people could attend – why would they come to mine? And besides, no one does Circles! Maybe they think I'm weird or have gone completely off the rails. Or, perhaps they just think I'm an outright imposter. What was I even thinking? I couldn't do this. I was assaulted by negativity and each thought shrunk me further.

Three women came to Circle that night. I felt ridiculous and fearful and like my wounded ego was in full control. I figured these three women would be disappointed too. I internalized it as a failure before I even let myself enjoy the success of my bravery. I associated the lack of attendance as to how the others felt about me. Surely, they didn't care since I was clearly not worth their time. Yet, despite the raw ache in my heart and the tears that I held back, we sat in Circle. I felt uncomfortable in this new skin, engaging for the first time in a space that intrigued yet challenged me. Here, I got to see my deeper nature more clearly: the magical being within me that had been set aside and suppressed as a child and was now ready to rise.

Since that time, Circle's monthly attendance hasn't grown much bigger – but it's still thriving – even when I've taken it online. Some people come every month and other people come when they can. There are those it serves for a short period of time, and those it serves for longer stretches. But no matter who comes, it offers people a space to meet themselves. Each time, the community connects with such authenticity, respect, and reverence that it humbles me. I've witnessed profound healing and revelation, hearts opening and egos dissolving, and the most beautiful, sacred connections emerging naturally between people on the path. The resonance we create here in this space is palpable, magical, and potent.

What is moving and powerful is the depth of sisterhood and witness available. To show up and express fears, grievances, and desires that don't have anywhere else to go. To see women show up as raw, whole, and alive even when it hurts or when the rest of the world has turned away. Circle has space for it all. Circle has space for what wants to be seen and named, for what wants to be loved and nourished. Holding this space has transformed my life and community from the inside out, and it has required so little time and energy in the bigger scheme of things. Yet it has given me so much.

Circle held a loving, non-judgmental space for me when Barrington died, through the intense online trolling that followed my first viral video, through my ego death and dark night of the soul. The friendships that have emerged from Circle bring more to my life than I ever imagined possible. I had no idea what I was getting myself into when I first began this experiment. All I know is that I followed the calling when it said, "hold circle" and everything followed from that powerful intuitive message. It doesn't pay me a salary and it doesn't fit into the ideas I originally had about myself and the world. And that's the point – I don't need to define myself to a specific identity or role in order to be who I am and to be accepted fully.

I've held Circle with small groups of friends and with companies and groups wanting a more integrated approach. Both men and women have attended my circles. Circle is always profound and yet I am surprised each time by what emerges in this sacred space of connection and community. It is here that I have come to understand what community means, and what true kinship looks like beyond any apparent divides. We show up together to be seen in our vulnerability and rawness, our truth and our tenderness. We witness each other come back to the sovereignty of our true selves. Regardless of whether someone is sobbing or sharing a victory, we celebrate our presence together.

What Is Circle?

Sitting in a circle is a practice as old as humanity. For eons, people have been coming together to share and listen to one another's stories in the form of a circle. We gather around a bonfire in the same way that we sit around a teacher in preschool. We learn from one another in this space, and we are witness to the growth of each person's unique experience. If you're thinking this is elementary stuff, you are not alone! That's why the practice is so foundational to our sense of connection as humans: we start this process young, but we don't always sustain it as we age. Or worse – we disconnect from the intention around it. Circle is important because it unites people in a moment of togetherness. Whatever the struggle or celebration, there is something for everyone to walk away with and information that will change them. Circle is a framework that eases communication and boosts collaboration because it's so healing and equalizing.

Everyone is welcome in Circle. All our experiences can be received here. That is why the container feels so sacred: we have the opportunity to be unconditionally accepted by our community, chosen or otherwise. As the circle represents totality and wholeness, we sit in Circle to symbolically represent that idea of sovereignty: original perfection. You are who you are. There is no hierarchy in Circle. I facilitate and guide, but I don't control the conversation or force the outcome. That is for the group to create through our shared experiences and interactions.

Circle is about creating resonance: the space to share, and the time to integrate meaning and insight so that we can benefit from the lessons revealed. This isn't therapy, in case you're wondering! This is a field of resonance between peers who are not attempting to fix or minimize anyone else's experience. Instead, we hold space for what is arising. There is power and strength in the vulnerable expression that can emerge here. We can more fully appreciate what is unique about each person and learn about ourselves through their journey. Together, we practice being open without judgment or shame.

I find that creating clear agreements to guide our interactions helps set a safe container for expression and honesty. For instance, in Circle I request that we don't cross-talk or interrupt, and that we honor and allow each person to share in full. We don't offer feedback or fix things. We just listen and receive – it turns out that is healing in and of itself. Circle is a way to be supported, even in ways that we didn't anticipate! And especially when we were afraid to ask for it.

There is an epidemic of loneliness on our planet and many of us feel isolated and alone in the deep inner work. In a recent survey that asked people how many trusted confidants they had in their lives who they could confide in, the most common response was "zero." In fact, a lack of social connection is a greater risk factor for early death than smoking! Many people feel shame or self-judgment that prevents them from reaching out to others and inviting them in. I know several leaders who don't feel safe to share their own doubts, frustrations, and insecurities with others for fear that they won't be held in the same respect or authority. Yet building relationships is at the heart of *all* goodness, and that includes business. Clients and partners choose you based on the simple fact that they trust you – *that* is value you can't purchase. Many people feel disconnected in their personal *and* professional lives and are struggling to find methods that feel human again. This is why Circle is even more necessary now.

I like to host Circle around the New Moon, but at the beginning of any new cycle is powerful. It is a time to talk about endings and new beginnings, what is being released and what is being called in now. Companies can use Circle as a way to facilitate honest conversations about key issues and ideas. Research has shown that circular formations in workshops and other kinds of discussion encourage an attitude of support and to-getherness, whereas a typical rectangular boardroom, for example, lends itself to a more top-down communication style.

A circular seating arrangement isn't hierarchical, so people are more likely to feel that they're valued. They're also more likely to feel comfortable sharing their ideas, as it's easier to contribute when you feel equal to others in the room. Also, this arrangement helps people feel that they're expected to contribute *because* their opinions are valid and valuable. Circle is a flexible framework that promotes community-building and a sense of belonging that transcends the personal *and* the professional.

Cultivating Authentic Connection and Expression

As social creatures who live most of our time in relationship to others, there is perhaps no need more important than authentic human interaction. As we discussed in the previous chapter, authenticity isn't just about speaking our minds or saying what we feel or think; it's creating a space for ourselves where all parts can come forward. It isn't about presenting the right face or saying the right thing. It's about acknowledging and accepting ourselves. Authenticity is where we move beyond the performance of the ego and into a space of deep alignment with our inner authority.

It becomes easier to cultivate a connection with ourselves and others because it is a natural outgrowth of your inner work and willingness to share. An authentic connection is one that stays open even after you've revealed your fears, doubts, and dirty skeletons. You'll know it's an authentic connection when you don't need to be fixed in order for that person to find you worthy or acceptable or lovable. This encourages each other to grow and step into those places that feel scary. We practice trusting ourselves, and we hold one another through the shaky moments.

Those who cannot bear witness to you in your unfolding are not in service to you. Those people who cannot make space for your authentic expression are not people who are committed to loving you unconditionally. Anyone who cannot accept you as you live into your power, express your truth, and evolve into your totality will hold you back and hold you down. True friendship and true love holds ever-expanding space for you to become as big as you desire. It exists as infinite love and abundance, infinite space and time for what wants to happen. Trust me when I say that there will be those who see you, who are ready for you, who want to ride with you on this journey. There are those people who are committed to meeting you, who are doing their inner work, and who are transforming alongside you. Those are the ones to welcome into your sovereign space. Some minor characters will come and go, and that's alright. There is a lesson in every connection, and some are only designed to be in your life for a short amount of time.

I have gained so much wisdom by witnessing others in their evolution. I have taken away profound lessons from other's challenges and applied these teachings to my own life and practice. It's in the reflections of others that I see myself from a different perspective. I have learned that asking for help is not a weakness. I've noticed who triggers me and how those triggers arise to show me where I have an open wound in need of healing. I have forgiven people whose actions cut me to the bone. I have found deeper intimacy and connection within all my relationships as a result. Knowing that I can create this sacred space for myself to be held has been the greatest gift of all. I am more empowered to show up for my life, for I know that no matter what happens I will be supported by my community. When I believe in myself and show up as *that* person, I become a light for others on the path of sovereignty.

Reflection Questions

1. Reflect on the cycles and rhythms in your life. What inspires you to begin a new cycle? Can you feel when a new cycle is beginning?

____

____

____

____

   a. How does the energy change throughout the course of a cycle in your life? For example, when you begin a new project, a new job, or a new relationship.

____

____

____

____

2. Who is part of your community? What does community mean to you? Does the word resonate with you? How do you participate in your community?

____

____

____

____

a. Who are the people in your life with whom you can be fully yourself? Who can you count on? Who do you turn to in times of deep need? With whom do you share your greatest joy?

____

____

____

____

3. Ask yourself the deep questions that invite your heart and soul to recognize our shared humanity. Questions like:

a. How can I express my individuality *and* still participate in a meaningful way as part of the collective?

____

____

____

____

b. What emotions or experiences of mine have I noticed recently in other people's stories? How do I react to them?

____

____

____

____

c. Am I willing to share the stories, lessons, and experiences that have hurt me? Who do I feel safe to share them with?

____

____

____

____

d. How can I step into a leadership role in my life? What does that look like in my personal community? In my professional career path? In my spiritual life?

____

____

____

____

Actionable Practices

1. Make a commitment to get out into nature. Plan different kinds of excursions that immerse you in the outdoors: visit National Parks or local parks, set up a kiddie pool in your backyard, plant flowers or water your garden by hand, walk around your neighborhood every morning. Notice how you feel in the mind, body, emotions, and inner landscape. Let your senses take in the subtle pleasures of being alive on this planet.

2. Apply the natural cycle phases to your Defining Moment with a call to notice the energetics throughout each phase:

   a. When did the situation (theme, idea, concept) begin? When did it "sprout"? How did it expand and grow? Did it feel like a new potential and possibility? What was the main theme?

   ____

   ____

   ____

   ____

   b. How did you take action to move toward what you desired? When did you encounter opposition, friction, or challenges?

   ____

   ____

   ____

   ____

c. How did you move past or work with any doubts, hesitations, and tensions? Did you get stuck or did you take empowered action?

____

____

____

____

d. When did you involve or connect with others? Who did you turn to and how did you communicate with them? How did you speak to yourself?

____

____

____

____

e. What brought forth the culmination of the theme? What happened to trigger the realization of the lesson, cycle, or situation?

____

____

____

____

f. What was the manifestation of the theme? When did it "bear fruit"? What were the results? What inner needs surfaced in your consciousness? How did you express, share or move forward?

____

____

____

____

g. How did you initiate new changes based on the manifestation/results and the lessons you learned? How did you, yourself, change?

____

____

____

____

h. What did you learn from the cycle? What did you assimilate and embody from this experience? What loose ends did you tie up in order to be complete? How did you prepare for the next cycle to come? What was seeded at this time?

____

____

____

____

3. Hold your own Circle. Call in your community. This can be as few as 1 other person.

   a. Create a space that feels sacred to you, adorn the space with some flowers, crystals, candles, or other items that meaningfully represent the energy you wish to call in.

   ____

   ____

   ____

   ____

   b. Welcome your participants to sit with you, take a few deep breaths together to settle in. Look each other in the eyes.

   ____

   ____

   ____

   ____

   c. Initiate the resonance by giving thanks to each participant for being with you, give thanks to any other elements or energies that you wish to invite into the circle – for example, the four directions, Mother Earth, the Stars, the Sun, etc.

   ____

   ____

   ____

d. Begin with an invitation to have each participant "check in" –ask them to introduce themselves and to describe in a few words how they are feeling.

____

____

____

____

e. Bring the topic of discussion forward – perhaps it is a new moon theme, or a celebration, or a completion. What is the general topic and energy that wants to be contemplated and shared?

____

____

____

____

f. Invite each participant to share what comes up for them if they feel called to do so. As each participant shares, the others will hold space, silently and intently listening as each person is able to vocalize and express themselves. Try not to offer advice, solutions, or anything that resembles a "fix."

____

____

____

____

g. Express gratitude to each participant for sharing their experience, thoughts, and feelings. Honor them for where they are, and who they are.

____

____

____

____

h. Close the circle by giving thanks to the energies that were called in, to the participants, and to all that was shared in Circle. Look each other in the eyes again, and give thanks to your community for coming together in resonant space.

____

____

____

____

Go Deeper

- *The Hero With a Thousand Faces* by Joseph Campbell

- *Man's Search for Meaning* by Viktor A. Frankl

- Lunar Planning Tools and Apps such as *LunarPlanner.com*

A Final Note: Calling In Your Highest Intention

S tand for a second and take yourself in. Look back at who you were when you started and who you are now. From the perspective of the spiral – ever-expanding – witness your journey thus far.

You are here to learn, to experience, to integrate, and to finally embody all that you are. Money, efficiency, and productivity are not the only metrics of success. Your choice to live attuned to your essence defines your output and outcomes. Your awareness reshapes everything. You have innate abilities that transcend your ideas of what is possible. Welcome all of this in.

You are the creator and creatrix of your life. It is yours to shape and mold. Where do you want to go with that power? This work is a lifelong practice. Sovereignty is our natural state. Self-empowerment is an operating system. Self-mastery is a lifestyle. As you take deeper steps to embody your wisdom, how do you desire to follow it? How will you let it lead you?

Goals are one way to define clear containers for your intentions. But what if your discipline became your devotion instead? Consider instead this invitation: what do you want to spend your time in devotion to? How do you want to worship yourself and your life? Goals will naturally arise when it is clear what you are committed to. What do your inner authority and authentic essence desire?

This is a subtle yet powerful distinction. Notice how your motivation changes when you align to devotion. Achievement does not need to arise from only directing your energy and attention into goal-setting. Centering yourself in a feeling of devotion helps clarify the goals, purpose, and meaning you seek to manifest and magnetize toward you.

My hope is that you are devoted to yourself moving forward. That you find joy in being here as you are. That your sovereign path becomes interwoven with your everyday so that they support one another at all times. That you step into your inner authority and express it effortlessly. If you haven't already, now is the time to commit to your path fully. Commit to yourself fully. Commit to rising up to meet your calling. Commit to your total sovereignty. Commit to supporting others in standing in their sovereignty. After all, it's a community effort to call each other forward into our highest expression.

Call upon your inner divine authority as the guide within. Start sitting with it daily and develop an ongoing, constant conversation with your source of truth: the powerful intuition that moves potential into productivity, and into form. You are your most powerful ally – and you always have been.

It's been a great honor to share my experiences and this space with you. Thank you for your presence and for walking this path with me. I bow deeply to you and your journey. I see you and I honor you. Finally, if there is one last thing I desire to impart – beyond all the stories and the science – it is the following invitation:

From My Divine
Authority to Yours:

Trust

Yourself.

Epilogue: The Power of Sharing Your Story

We know by now that telling stories is powerful. This fundamental form of human connection helps us pass on life lessons and wisdom to our communities and future generations. Though we may not gather around a bonfire as much as we once did, storytelling is imprinted in our psyche and social fabric.

The great human story has been documented prolifically by Joseph Campbell. He calls this the mono-myth; a cohesive and epic storyline that is both present in every story across cultures and history while transcending them all. The storyline is presented as a cycle – of course! – and is often referred to as the Hero's Journey. It is the archetypal journey that underlines all stories in a way: from the beginning, or call to adventure (i.e. planting the first seeds), to the climax (i.e. harvesting the fruit), to the completion and re-integration of the person after the journey. This last part is the gift to the community; for others will benefit and carry forward the learnings far into the future.

The root word of *authority* is author. You are the author of your story, with the power to define your narrative and choose the adventure you want to play out. When we bring awareness to any narrative, we get to shift it. In the same way, when you share a story with others, you control what details are emphasized and prioritized. We do this with our lives as well. How do you want to tell your story? Are you the hero who overcomes the obstacles and gains wisdom, knowledge, and strength? Or, are you the victim to whom life happens?

Telling your story to others might just be the most powerful medicine on this planet. When we honor ourselves, we are better able to honor others. When we accept ourselves, it becomes easier to accept others. When we are not afraid of ourselves, we are less afraid of what others present to us. And yet so many of us leave our stories untold, our songs unsung – and when this happens, we experience the pain of isolation: we feel lonely, listless, or out of touch with our life's purpose, plagued with a chronic sense that something is out of alignment. We all seek to express our individuality, our uniqueness, and we seek this reflection through others because we ultimately desire to feel like we belong. Yet belonging doesn't require you to change who you are; it requires you to *be* who you are.

Every time you tell your story and are truly heard, your body gets to relax. It flips off the stress hormones it's producing and releases endorphins and other hormones to help you heal instead. Not only does this turn on the body's innate self-repair mechanisms which function as preventative medicine, it also helps ameliorate feelings of depression, anxiety, fear, anger, and disconnection.

In sharing with one another, we disrupt the story that we are alone! It's as simple as that. Sometimes all it takes is reaching out to someone and expressing something true for us to start feeling seen and heard. The minute you discover that someone else is suffering just like you—or even better, that they're celebrating their wholeness just like you—that sense of disconnection eases and you start to glimpse the truth—that we are all connected and all on the path.

And if you think that what you have to say or to share is somehow not enough, let me remind you what one of my sisters from Circle once wrote to me: "The more random you think what you have to say might be, the more it may resonate if you just trust and put it out there. Just as an example, several things you shared with me from Circle have helped other people I have had conversations with this week and last week, in profound ways. It would take too long to explain in an email so just trust me when I say the ripple effects of your actions have been widespread and real."

By bravely sharing your truth, you call mirrors for truth to you. You allow others to experience the truth within you and respond with theirs. Stories are a form of healing. Whether we write them for ourselves, publish them, speak them, or simply share them with others in any format, we bring our humanity front and center. We invite and permit ourselves and others to be themselves; to be human, vulnerable, open, caring, compassionate and, when we need it most, forgiving. It's in the forgiving that we honor our humanity. As I honor myself by sharing my story, I honor you by opening myself to yours.

Compassionate Re-Experiencing

When we're living our life in the moment, we are playing our part and acting out our destiny. It requires self-reflection and self-inquiry to understand the meaning of those experiences. It requires the excavation on your end to surface the meaning and the Soul's lesson.

When we can go back to the moments that defined us and re-experience them through a much more compassionate lens, it is possible to discover buried treasure: details and insights that we passed over in our original assumptions because we were so invested in our story.

By remembering, reviewing, and reliving key defining moments in my life, I discovered that I could relive them without getting stuck in the story, which was often skewed by ego and emotion. Engaging with this process is like being an observer or an investigative journalist. I saw myself as a protagonist in the story, trying to make her way in the world. I tried on different perspectives and points of view now that I had the advantage of the passage of time and space away from the heat of the moment. I had a vantage point. I could get out of the weeds and do some clean-up because I was experiencing my life from a different place. I could change the way I remembered the past.

I uncovered the biggest source of pain that had been driving most of my life's experience, especially the experiences and situations that didn't turn out well, or that left me feeling unworthy, unloved, unacceptable, and without value. I uncovered the source of my buried shame – and I was able to do something about it. And the most amazing thing happened – all that emotion, once I felt it, and once I saw myself with different eyes – compassionate, understanding, forgiving – the emotions stopped triggering deep-seated, unconscious negative beliefs. It was as though I time traveled because something changed in me in the present moment. I felt lighter, better.

I undertook the most incredible, heart-opening, and intense process of self-realization through the practices of self-inquiry, self-reflection, and writing as I developed what I call Compassionate Re-Experiencing.

Even though I lived those experiences, I didn't fully understand the meaning of them until much later. I simply wasn't aware at the time. I was asleep at the wheel. I couldn't see the big picture, the patterns, or the outcomes when I was enmeshed within the storyline.

This process of Compassionate Re-Experiencing isn't always gentle. It stirs up a lot of feelings, both the joy and the pain. This process allows for an integration of soul fragments that have been buried under layers of shame, hurt, blame, anger, denial, and so on. We have all been shaped by our most challenging moments. We have been forged in strength through our difficulties. Compassionate Re-Experiencing offers us the opportunity to look back on ourselves and our life with a new perspective and to rewrite our role as the hero or heroine.

The Process of Compassionate Re-Experiencing

Reflecting on the defining moments in your life with objectivity and compassion helps you see the soul wisdom showing you where you were meant to go. Compassionate Re-Experiencing teaches you to safely go into the archive of your life's experience and clear out the emotional chaos that you're still carrying with you.

In every moment and situation, we are acting out our free-will through choice. We're also playing out unconscious behavior and programming. Reflection and self-inquiry are necessary in order to understand and extract the meaning of those experiences. With Compassionate Re-Experiencing, you are making changes in your past, present, *and* future simultaneously. When you view your past self with compassion, you instantly create a more loving and empowering state in the present. After all, you are practicing acceptance! From this present state, you make more aligned actions that will play out in your future. Through this process, you are "wholing" yourself, which is another way of saying you are *healing* yourself.

This exercise is a written exercise that examines our defining moments. I recommend approaching this like you were writing a memoir of a significant event in your life. This is not for anyone else to read; this is only for you.

1. Start by preparing a special space to write. What do you need to do in order to feel supported in your inner work? Consider setting aside an area for your sacred work and decorating it with personal talismans and totems that inspire you or remind you of your worth, power, and potential.

____

____

____

2. Meditate or reflect on the most significant event in your *adult* life where you decided to initiate a change that you *needed* to make. This wasn't a quick or easy decision; you didn't take it lightly. It had far-reaching consequences that extended beyond you. It might have taken you years to make it. Perhaps it went against convention, against what others expected of you, or against what you thought you were capable of doing. This decision might have caused emotional

pain, presented various challenges and changes, and ultimately led you in a new, potentially life-changing direction.

____

____

____

____

3. Once you've identified this event, write it down: i.e. "Leaving my marriage" or "Starting my business" or "Facing an illness." Now, reflect on the story you told yourself about this experience up until now. What words go through your mind? What emotions come up? What is the theme of your story and how does it make you feel?

____

____

____

____

4. Write out this version of what happened and label it the "Old Story" when you're done. Set it aside.

____

____

____

____

5. Ask yourself: What was your "lightning strike" – the moment you *knew* something needed to change? Give yourself some time to sit with this question and see what emotions or memories come up.

____

____

____

____

6. Now, re-watch this situation as though it is happening to someone else, not you. See this person and be with their experience, as though you were relating to a character in a film. Get clear on what exactly this person was feeling and experiencing when the lightning bolt struck. Allow yourself to feel any trapped emotions that come up – that's essential to this exercise! Let them flow through and out. Imagine you are helping this old self by feeling what they couldn't feel then. Name the emotions. Can you identify any negative or disempowering beliefs within them?

____

____

____

____

7. Now it's time to write it out! Imagine you are narrating the climactic scene of a movie. Explore the following questions as you do so:

a. What was the lesson the hero/ine learned?

____

____

____

____

b. Underneath all the emotions and storytelling, what is the truth that wants to be witnessed?

____

____

____

____

c. What themes are present in this situation?

____

____

____

____

d. What characters are involved? What other actors facilitated or played a role in the unfolding of the situation?

____

____

____

____

e. What role did your intuition play? Did you heed it or did you ignore it? Which intelligence centers were active and how did they communicate to you?

____

____

____

____

8. Once you've re-experienced that situation, take a moment to acknowledge the choice you had in that situation. Notice and release any emotional back-talk, or what scientists call "internal disinhibition" – the thoughts and feelings that derailed you from making other choices. Offer your gratitude for the teachings it led you to – and to yourself for making a necessary if difficult choice.

9. Finally, do a quick inventory of decisions you made based on that moment.

a. What did you do afterward? What came next?

____

____

____

____

b. What future decisions were influenced by this moment?

____

351

____

____

____

c. What did you learn about yourself and how did you change as a result?

____

____

____

____

Sharing Stories of Inner Authority

If you are feeling called to share your learnings with me and possibly with others, then I invite you to send me your story so that your journey can impact and open the way for future conscious leaders.

I invite anyone who feels ready to stand in their truth to share a written or video story that shares a pivotal defining moment. Use the exercise above as your template to frame your insights. Once you have a clear and concise story to share with the world, please send me your Inner Authority Defining Moment at: dm@productiveintuition.com.

Appreciation

To Katharine Hargreaves, for walking the Warrior Priestess path alongside me and helping bring this wisdom, and my story, to these pages.

To Shauna Bergh, for your compassionate insights into the workings of the psyche and the complexity of being a whole, complex, human being.

To Ashley Turner, for walking with me through the portal and onto the Priestess path.

To Kimberly, Erica & Hari, for being the first Sisters to Circle of Sovereignty and for your continued love and support throughout my flourishing.

To my Sisters, and all those who have been in Circle, for trusting me to hold spaces as we created a heartfelt community and flourished together.

To my family, for always believing I could make a meaningful contribution to this World.

To Andrew, for being a mirror to my process, willing to step into the work of conscious expansion with me, and for honoring the wild, the fierce, and the tender forces that course through me.

To the Subtle Realms, for your ever-present love, patience and support.

About the Author

AdaPia d'Errico is a modern mystic and business-woman. As a visionary leader with 20+ years of experience across countries, cultures, and corporate and start-up environments, she integrates ambition and wisdom with the highest definition of integrity. AdaPia has co-founded businesses, launched brands, and redefined industries. As a respected entrepreneur and executive who embodies vulnerability and resilience, when AdaPia speaks, people are impacted. Her masterful storytelling catapulted her to viral success when one of her videos reached over 35 million views parentheses (and counting). In her first book, AdaPia is coming down from the proverbial mountain to share profound insights and personal stories on how she has cultivated her intuition to guide her through her greatest success and challenges. Her heartfelt passion for self-mastery represents a new vision for leadership based on personal sovereignty in service to others.

FOR EVEN MORE SUPPORT ON HOW TO
INTEGRATE YOUR INTUITION AND
ACTIVATE YOUR INNER AUTHORITY,
GO TO PRODUCTIVEINTUITION.COM

Made in the USA
Columbia, SC
02 April 2021

35496297R00212